The Life

and Miracles

of

St Benedict

by
St Gregory the Great

ISBN-13: 978-1977983220

ISBN-10: 1977983227

St Athanasius Press
2017

Specializing in Reprinting Catholic Classics!

PAX
ROME
1895.

To His Eminence
LUCIDO MARIA PAROCCHI
Cardinal Bishop of Albano
Vicar General of His Holiness
POPE LEO XIII.

This Edition
of the
Life and rule of Saint Benedict
is
respectfully, gratefully and affectionately
dedicated
by
His English Daughters in Rome
who owe to His Eminence
more graces and blessings
than words can convey.

The Latin of this edition of the life of St. Benedict by St. Gregory
the Great, is from that used by dom. Edmund Mart`ane, the English is
almost exactly that of the quaint translation published in 1638. The
text used for the Holy Rule is that of an ancient MS. existing at Monte
Cassino, first published in 1659 by Dom. Paul de Ferrariis, a monk of
that Abbey. The English is, as far as is consistent with the original,
from the time honoured translation of 1638, as edited in 1875 by "one
of the Benedictine Fathers of St. Michael's, near Hereford."

CONTENTS

INTRODUCTION.

THERE was a man of venerable life, Benedict by name and grace, who from the time of his very childhood carried the heart of an old man. His demeanour indeed surpassing his age, he gave himself no disport or pleasure, but living here upon earth he despised the world with all the glory thereof, at such time as he might have most freely enjoyed it. He was born in the province of Nursia of honourable parentage and sent to Rome to study the liberal sciences. But when he saw there many through the uneven paths of vice run headlong to their own ruin, he drew back his foot, but new-set in the world, lest, in the search of human knowledge, he might also fall into the same dangerous precipice.

Contemning therefore learning and studies and abandoning his father's house and goods, he desired only to please God in a virtuous life. Therefore he departed skilfully ignorant and wisely unlearned. I have not attained unto all this man did, but the few things which I here set-down, were related to me by four of his disciples; namely, Constantine, a very reverend man, who succeeded him in the government of the Monastery; Valentinian, who for many years bore rule in the Monastery of Lateran; Simplicius, who was the third superior of that congregation after him; and Honoratus who yet governeth the Monastery which he first inhabited.

CHAPTER I.

Benedict having now left the schools resolved to betake himself to the desert, accompanied only by his nurse who most tenderly loved him. Coming therefore to a place called Affile, and remaining for some time in the Church of St. Peter by the charitable invitement of many virtuous people who lived there for devotion, so it chanced that his nurse borrowed of a neighbour a sieve to cleanse wheat, which being left carelessly upon the table was found broken in two pieces. Therefore on her return finding it broke, she began to weep bitterly because it was only lent her. But the religious and pious boy, Benedict, seeing his nurse lament was moved with compassion, and taking with him the two pieces of the broken sieve, with tears he gave himself to prayer, which no sooner ended, but he found the sieve whole, and found not any sign that it had been broken. Then presently he restored the sieve which had been broken, whole to his nurse, to her exceeding comfort. This matter was divulged unto all that lived thereabout, and so much admired by all, that the inhabitants of that place caused the sieve to be hanged up in the Church porch, that not only those present, but all posterity might know with how great gifts of grace Benedict had been endowed from the beginning of his conversion. The sieve remained to be seen for many years after, and hung over the Church door even until the times of the Longobards.

But Benedict more desirous to suffer afflictions than covetous of praise; and rather willing to undergo labours for the honour of God, than to be extolled with the favours of this world, fled secretly from his nurse to a remote place in the desert called Subiaco, distant about forty miles from Rome, in which a fountain springing with cool and crystal waters, extendeth itself at first into a broad lake, and running farther with increase of waters becometh at the last a river.

As he was travelling to this place, a certain monk called Romanus met him and asked whither he was going. Having understood his intention, he both kept it secret and afforded him help, moreover he gave him a religious habit and assisted him in all things. The man of God being come to this place lived for the space of three years in an obscure cave, unknown to any man except Romanus the Monk, who lived not far off in a Monastery governed by Father Deodatus. But he would piously steal forth, and on certain days bring to Benedict a loaf of

9

bread which he had spared from his own allowance. But there being
no way to the cave from Romanus his cell by reason of a steep and
high rock which hung over it, Romanus used to let down the loaf by
a long cord to which also he fastened a little bell, that by the sound of
it, the man of God might know when Romanus brought him the bread,
and going out may receive it. But the old enemy, envying the charity of the one and the refection of the other, when on a certain day he
beheld the bread let down in this manner, threw a stone and brake the
bell. Notwithstanding,Romanus afterwards failed not to assist him in
the best manner he was able. Now when it pleased Almighty God that
Romanus should rest from his labours, and that the life of Benedict
should be manifest to the world for an example to all men, that the
candle set upon a candlestick might shine and give light to the whole
Church of God, our Lord vouchsafed to appear to a certain Priest living far off, who had make ready his dinner for Easter Day, saying to
him: "Thou hast prepared good cheer for thyself, and My servant in
such a place is famished for hunger." Who presently rose up, and on
the solemn day of Easter went towards the place with such meat as
he had provided for himself, where seeking the man of God, amongst
craggy rocks, winding valleys and hollow pits he found him hid in
a cave. Then after prayers, and blessing the Almighty Lord, they sat
down, and after some spiritual discourse the Priest said: "Rise, and let
us take our refection, for this is Easter Day." To whom the man of God
answered: "I know it is Easter, because I have found so much favour
as to see thee." (For not having a long time conversed with men, he
did not know it was Easter Day.) The good Priest did therefore again
affirm it, saying: "Truly this is the day of our Lord's Resurrection, and
therefore it is not fit that you should keep abstinence, and for this cause
I am sent that we may eat together that which Almighty God hath bestowed on us." Whereupon blessing God, they fell to their meat. Their
discourse and dinner ended, the Priest returned to his Church.

About the same time certain shepherds found him hid in a cave; who,
at the first, spying him among the bushes, clothed in the skins of
beasts, took him for some wild beast, but afterwards knowing him to
be a servant of God, many of them were converted from their savage
life to virtue. By this means his name began to be famous in the country, and many did resort unto him, bringing with them necessaries for
his body, while they received from his lips the food of life.

CHAPTER II.

How he overcame a temptation of the flesh.

The holy man being on a certain day alone, the tempter was at hand; for a little black bird, commonly called an ousel, began to fly about his face, and that so near as the holy man, if he would might have taken it with his hand; but no sooner had he made the sign of the cross than the bird vanished. When presently so great a carnal temptation assailed him, that before the holy man had never felt the like. For the remembrance of a woman which some time he had seen, was so lively represented to his fancy by the wicked spirit, and so vehemently did her image inflame his breast with lustful desires, that almost overcome by pleasure, he was determining to leave the wilderness. But suddenly assisted with divine grace he came to himself, and, seeing near him a thicket full of nettles and briars, he threw off his garments and cast himself naked into the midst of those sharp thorns and nettles, where he rolled himself so long, that, when he rose up, all his body was pitifully rent; thus by the wounds of his flesh he cured those of his soul, by turning pleasure into pain; and by the vehemence of outward torments he extinguished the unlawful flame which burnt within overcoming sin by changing the fire. After which time, as he himself related to his disciples, he was so free from the like temptation, that he never felt any such motion.

Many after this began to forsake the world and to hasten to put themselves under his government. Being now altogether free from vice, he worthily deserved to be made a master of virtue. As it is commanded by Moses that the Levites should serve from five and twenty years and upward, and after fifty years they should be appointed to keep the holy vessels.

PETER.

I have already understood something of this testimony alleged, yet I pray make it more plain unto me.

GREGORY.

It is manifest, Peter, that in youth the temptations of the flesh are great, but after fifty natural heat waxeth cold: now the souls of good men are the holy vessels. Therefore while the elect are in temptation, it is necessary that they live under obedience, and be wearied with labours, but when, by reason of their age, the fervour of temptations is assuaged, they are ordained keepers of holy vessels, that is become instructors of souls.

PETER.

I confess what you say has given me full satisfaction, and therefore this place of Scripture being clearly expounded, I pray you hasten on with the holy man's life which you have begun.

CHAPTER III.

How St. Benedict brake a glass by the sign of the cross.

Having thus vanquished this temptation, the man of God like a good soil well manured and weeded, brought forth abundant fruit of the seed of virtue, so that his fame began to spread itself more largely. Not far off was a Monastery, whose Abbot being dead, the whole Convent repaired to the venerable man Benedict, and with earnest persuasions requested him for their Abbot, which he refused for a long time, fore-warning them that his manner of life and theirs were not agreeable; yet at length overcome with importunity he gave consent. But when in the same Monastery he began to observe regular discipline, so that none of the Monks (as in former time) were permitted by their disorder to swerve any way form the path of virtue, which receiving they fell into a great rage, and began accusing themselves of their choice in receiving him for a Superior, whose integrity of life was disproportionate to their perverseness.

And therefore, when they perceived themselves restrained from unlawful acts, it grieved them to leave their desires, and hard it was to relinquish old customs and begin a new life, besides the conversation of good men is always odious to the wicked, they began therefore to plot his death, and after consultation had together, they poisoned his wine. So when the glass which contained the empoisoned drink was, according to the custom of the Monastery, presented at table to be blessed by the Abbot, Benedict putting forth his hand and making the sign of the Cross, the glass which was held far off brake in pieces, as if instead of blessing the vase of death, he had thrown a stone against it. By this the man of God perceived that the glass had in it the drink of death which could not endure the sign of life. So presently rising up with a mild countenance and tranquil mind, having called the Brethren together, he thus spake unto them: "Almighty God of His mercy forgive you, Brethren, why have you dealt thus with me? Did not I foretell you that my manner of life and yours would not agree? Go, and seek a Superior to your liking; for you can have me no longer with you." This said, he forthwith returned to the solitude he loved so well, and lived there with himself, in the sight of Him who seeth all things.

PETER.

I do not well understand what you mean: "He lived with himself."

GREGORY.

If the holy man had been longer constrained to govern those who had unanimously conspired against him, and were so contrary to him in life and manners, it might, peradventure, have diminished his own vigour and fervour of devotion, withdrawing his mind from the light of contemplation. So that over much busied in correcting the faults of others, he might have neglected his own; and so perhaps lost himself, and yet not gained others. For as often as by contagious motions we are transported out of ourselves we remain the same, but not with ourselves, because not looking into our own actions, we are wandering about other things. For do we think that he was with himself who went into a far country, consumed the portion allotted to him, and, after he had put himself into the service of a citizen of that country, kept his hogs, and was glad to eat the husks which they are: notwithstanding, when he began to consider what he had lost, as the Scripture testifieth: "Being come to himself, he said: how many hirelings in my father's house have plenty of bread." If, therefore, he were before with himself, how was it true that he returned to himself?

I may well say, therefore, that his holy man lived with himself, because he never turned the eye of his soul from himself, but standing always on his guard with great circumspection, he kept himself continually in the all-seeing eye of his Creator.

PETER.

How is it then to be understood, which is written of the Apostle Peter, when he was led by the Angel out of the prison? Who returning to himself said: "Now I know assuredly that the Lord hath sent his Angel, and hath delivered me out of the hands of Herod, and from all the expectation of the people of the Jews."

GREGORY.

Two ways, Peter, we are carried out of ourselves: for either by sinfulness of thought we fall beneath ourselves, or by the grace of contemplation we are raised above ourselves. He therefore, that kept the hogs, by his inconstancy of mind and uncleanness, fell beneath himself: but he, whom the Angel loosed and ravished into an ecstasy, was indeed out of himself, but yet above himself. But both of them returned to themselves, the one when, reclaiming his lewd life, he was converted at heart, the other when from the height of contemplation, he returned to his natural and ordinary understanding. Thus venerable Benedict in that solitude dwelt with himself, for as much as he kept himself within his thoughts: for as often as by the fervour of contemplation he was elevated, without doubt he left himself as it were beneath himself.

PETER.

I like well this you say but resolve me, I pray you, should he have left those Monks of whom he had once taken charge?

GREGORY.

In my opinion, Peter, a bad community may be tolerated where there are found at least some good which may be helped. But where there is no benefit to be expected of any good, labour is many times lost upon the bad. Especially if there be any present occasions wherein we may do God better service. Now whom was there whom the holy man should have stayed to govern, when they had all conspired against him? And many things are considered by the soul of the perfect which ought not to be passed in silence, for they, perceiving their endeavours to be without effect, depart to some other place, there to employ themselves more profitably.

Wherefore that famous preacher who desired to be dissolved and to be with Christ, unto whom to live is Christ, and to die is gain, did not only desire himself to suffer, but did also animate others to do the like. He being persecuted at Damascus, caused himself to be let down from the wall by a cord and basket whereby he escaped privately. Shall we say then that Paul feared death which he earnestly desired for the love of Christ, as appeareth by his own testimony? But as he foresaw that his endeavours there would profit little, with much difficulty he reserved himself to labour in another place with better success. For this valiant champion of God would not be confined to so narrow limits, but sought battles in the open field. So you may observe that the venerable Benedict, left not so many incorrigible in that place as he converted to a spiritual life elsewhere.

PETER.

You say true, as both reason and the example alleged prove, but I pray return to prosecute the life of this holy Father.

GREGORY.

The holy man for many years in that desert increased wonderfully in virtues and miracles, whereby a great number in those parts were gathered together in the service of Almighty God: so that, by the assistance of our Lord Jesus Christ, he built there twelve monasteries, in each of which he put twelve Monks with their superiors, and retained a few with himself whom he thought to instruct further.

Now began divers noble and devout personages from Rome to resort to him, and commended their children to be brought up by him in the service of Almighty God. At the same time, Equitius brought unto him Maurus, and Tertullus a Senator his son Placidus, both very hopeful children, of which two, Maurus, although young, yet by reason of his forwardness in the school of virtue, began to assist his master, but Placidus was as yet a child of tender years.

CHAPTER IV.

How he reclaimed an indevout Monk.

In one of those Monasteries which he had built thereabout, was a certain Monk that could not stay at his prayers, but, so soon as he saw his brethren kneel and dispose themselves for their mental prayer, he would go out, and there spend his wandering thoughts upon worldly and transitory things. For which, having been often admonished by his Abbot, he was brought before the man of God, who also sharply reprehended him for his folly; but, returning to his Monastery, he scarce remembered two days what the man of God had said to him, for the third day he fell to his old custom, and at the time of prayer went out again: whereof when the servant of God was informed by the Abbot the second time, he said: "I will come myself and reform him." And when he was come to the same Monastery, and the Brethren after the Psalms ended, at the accustomed time betook themselves to prayer, he perceived a little black boy, who pulled this Monk (who could not remain at his prayers) out by the hem of his garment. This he insinuated secretly to Pompeianus Abbot of the Monastery, and to Maurus: "See you hot there who it is that draweth this Monk out?" Who answered, "No." "Let us pray", replied he, "that you may likewise see whom this Monk followeth." After prayer continued for two days, Maurus the monk saw, but Pompeianus the Abbot of the Monastery could not perceive anything.

The next day when the man of God had finished his prayer he went out of the Oratory, and found the Monk standing without, whom he forthwith strake with a wand, and from that time ever after the Monk was free form the wicked suggestion of the black boy, and remained constant at his prayers. For the old enemy, as if himself had been beaten with the whip, dared no more to take command of his thoughts.

CHAPTER V.

How by the prayer of the man of God a spring issued from the top of a mountain.

Three of the Monasteries, which he founded in that place, were built upon the cliffs of a mountain, which was very troublesome to the Monks always to be forced to descend to the lake to fetch up their water, for, on account of the steepness of the mountain side, it was very difficult and dangerous to descend. Hereupon the Brethren of these three Monasteries came together to the servant of God Benedict saying: "It is very troublesome to us to have daily to go down for water as far as the lake, and therefore the Monasteries must of necessity be removed to some more commodious place." He dismissed them with comfortable words, and at night with little Placidus, whom we mentioned before, went up to the rock and there prayed a long time. Having ended his prayers, he put three stones for a mark in the same place, and so unknown to all he returned to his Monastery. Next day, when the Brethren came again to him for want of water he said: "Go, and on the rock where you shall find three stones one upon another, dig a little, for Almighty God is able to make water spring from the top of that mountain, that you may be eased of this labour." When they had made a hollow in that place, it was immediately filled with water, which issueth forth so plentifully that to this day it continueth running down to the floor of the mountain.

CHAPTER VI.

How the iron head of a bill from the bottom of the water returned to the handle again.

At another time, a certain Goth poor of spirit, desirous to lead a religious life, repaired to the man of God, Benedict, who most willingly received him. One day he ordered a bill to be given to him to cut up brambles in a place which he intended for a garden. This place, which the Goth had undertaken to accommodate, was over the lake's side.

While the Goth laboured amain in the cutting up the thick briars, the iron, slipping out of the handle, fell into the lake in a place so deep, that there was no hope to recover it. The Goth, having lost his bill, ran trembling to the Monk Maurus, and told him the mischance, confessing his fault penitently, who presently advertised Benedict the servant of God thereof. Immediately the man of God came himself to the lake, took the haft out of the Goth's hand, and cast it into the lake, when, behold, the iron rose up from the bottom and entered into the haft as before. Which he there rendered to the Goth saying: "Behold! work on and be not discomforted."

CHAPTER VII.

How his disciple Maurus walked on the water.

One day as venerable Benedict was in his cell, the aforesaid young Placidus, a Monk of the holy man, went out to the lake to fetch water, and letting down the bucket to take up water, by chance fell in himself after it, and was presently carried away by the stream, a bow's shoot from the side. This accident was at the same time revealed to the man of God in his cell, who quickly called Maurus, saying: "Run, brother Maurus, for the child who went to fetch water is fallen into the lake, and the stream hath carried him a great way." A wonderful thing and not heard of since the time of Peter the Apostle! Maurus having asked and received his benediction, upon the command of his Superior went forth in haste, and, being come to the place to which the child was driven by the stream, thinking still he went upon the dry land, he ran upon the water, took him by the hair of the head, and returned speedily back. No sooner had he set foot upon firm ground but he came to himself, and perceiving that he had gone upon the water, much astonished, he wondered how he had done that which wittingly he durst not adventure.

So, returning to his Superior, he related what had happened, which the venerable man Benedict ascribed to Maurus his prompt obedience, and not to his own merits; but contrariwise Maurus attributed it wholly to his command, not imputing any virtue to himself in that which he had done unwittingly. This humble and charitable contention, the child who was saved, was to decide, for he said: "When I was drawn out of the water, me thought I saw my Abbot's garments over my head and imagined that he had drawn me out."

PETER.

These are wonderful things you report, and may be to the edification of many: for my own part, the more I drink of this good man's miracles, the more I thirst.

CHAPTER VIII.

Of the poisoned loaf which the crow carried away.

When, as now, the places far and wide were very zealous in the love of our Lord God Jesus Christ, many abandoning the vanities of the world and putting themselves under the sweet yoke of our Redeemer; as it is the custom of the wicked to repine at the virtues of others, which themselves desire not to follow, one Florentius, the Priest of a Church hard by, and grandfather to Florentius our subdeacon, began by the instigation of the devil to be envious of the virtuous proceedings of the holy man, to derogate from his course of living hindering also as many as he could from resorting to him. But seeing that he could not stop his progress, the fame of his virtues still more increasing, and many upon the report of his sanctity reforming their lives daily, he became more and more envious, and constantly grew worse, for he desired himself the commendations of Benedict's life, but would not live commendably. Thus, blinded with envy, he sent to the servant of Almighty God a poisoned loaf for an offering, which the man of God received thankfully, although he was not ignorant of the poison in it. There used to come to him at the time of dinner a crow from the next forest, which took bread from his hand. Coming therefore, as she was wont, the man of God case before her the bread that the Priest had sent him, saying: "In the name of the Lord Jesus Christ take this bread and cast it in some place where no man may find it." The crow, gaping and spreading her wings, run croaking about it, as though she would have said, I would willingly fulfil thy command, but I am not able. The man of God commanded again saying: "Take it up, take it up, and cast it where no man may find it." So at length the crow took it up in her beak and flew away with it and three hours after returned again to receive from his hand her ordinary allowance. But the venerable Father, seeing the Priest so perversely bent to seek his life, was more sorry for him than grieved for himself. When the aforesaid Florentius saw that he could not kill the body of his master, he attempted what he could against the souls of his disciples, in so much that he sent seven naked girls into the garden of the Cloister where Benedict lived, that so playing for a long time hand in hand, they might entice their souls to naughtiness, which when the holy man espied out of his cell, to prevent the fall of his younger disciples, and considering that all this was done only for the persecuting of himself, he gave place to envy, and after he had disposed of the Oratories and other buildings, leaving in them a competent number of Brethren with Superiors, he took with him a few monks and removed to another place. Thus the man of God with humility avoided his hatred, whom Almighty God struck with a terrible judgment: for when the aforesaid Priest, standing in his summer house, heard to his great joy, that Benedict was gone, the room wherein he was fell down and crushed and killed the enemy of Benedict, all the rest of the house remaining immovable. This Maurus, the disciple of the man of God, thought fit to signify forthwith to the venerable Father Benedict, who was yet scarce gone ten miles saying: "Return for the Priest that did persecute you is slain." Which the man of God hearing took very heavily, both because his enemy was dead and because his disciple rejoiced thereat. Whereupon he enjoined him a penance for presuming in a joyful manner to bring such news to him.

PETER.

These are wonderful strange things which thou sayest. For in the drawing water out of a rock me thinks I behold in him Moses; in raising the iron from the bottom of the water he representeth Eliseus; in walking on the water Peter; in the obedience of the crow I conceive him another Elias; in bewailing his enemy's death I see David. In my opinion, this man was filled with the spirit of all the just.

GREGORY.

The man of God, Benedict, had in him, Peter, the spirit of God alone, which by the grace of free redemption replenished the hearts of all the elect, of which St. John saith: "There was true light which illuminateth every man that cometh into this world." Of which again it is written: "Of his plentitude and fulness we have all received." For the holy ones of God could indeed receive graces from God, but they could not impart them to others. He then gave signs of power to the lowly, who promised that He would shew the miracle of Jonas to His enemies, deigning in their sight to die, and in the sight of the humble to arise. So that the one should have what they would contemn, and the other what reverence and love. By which mystery it came to pass, that while the proud were spectators of His ignominious death, the humble contrariwise, against death, lay hold of the power of His glory.

PETER.

But declare, I pray, whither the holy man removed or if he wrought miracles in any other place?

GREGORY.

The holy man by removing changed his habitation, but not his adversary. For afterwards he endured so much the more grievous battles, by how much he had now the master of wickedness fighting openly against him.

The castle called Cassino is situated upon the side of a high mountain, which containeth as it were, in the lap thereof, the same castle, and riseth into the air three miles high so that the top seemeth to touch the very heavens: on this stood an old temple where Apollo was worshipped by the foolish country people, according to the custom of the ancient heathens. Round about it, likewise, grew groves, in which even until that time, the mad multitude of infidels offered their idolatrous sacrifices. The man of God coming to that place brake down the idol, overthrew the altar, burnt the groves, and, of the temple of Apollo, made a chapel to St. Martin, and, where the profane altar had stood, he built a chapel of St. John; and, by continual preaching, converted many of the people thereabout. But the old enemy not bearing this silently, did present himself, not covertly or in a dream but openly and visibly in the sight of the Father, and with great cries complained of the violence he suffered, in so much that the brethren heard him though they could see nothing. For, as the venerable Father told his disciples, the wicked fiend represented himself to his sight all on fire, and, with flaming mouth and flashing eyes, seemed to rage against him. And, then, they all heard what he said, for, first, he called him by his name, and, when the man of God would make him no answer, he fell to reviling him. And whereas before he cried: "Benedict, Benedict," and saw he could get no answer, then he cried: "Maledict, not Benedict, what hast thou to do with me, and why dost thou persecute me?" But now we shall behold new assaults of the old enemy against the servant of God, against whom willingly did he make war, but against his will did he give him occasions of many victories.

23

CHAPTER IX.

How the man of God by his prayer, removed a huge stone.

One day, as the brethren were building the cells of the Cloister, there lay a stone in the midst which they determined to lift up and put into the building. When two or three were not able to move it, they set more to it, but it remained as immoveable as if it had been held by roots to the ground, so that it was easy to conceive that the old enemy sat upon it, since that so many men were not able to lift it. After much labour in vain, they sent to the man of God to help them with his prayers to drive away the enemy, who presently came, and having first prayed, he gave his blessing, when behold the stone was as easily lifted as if it had not weight at all.

CHAPTER X.

Of the fantastical fire which burned the kitchen.

Then the man of God thought good that they should dig in that place. When they had entered a good deepness, the Brethren found a brazen idol, which happening for the present to be cast in the kitchen, suddenly there seemed a flame to rise out of it, and, to the sight of all the Monks it appeared that all the kitchen was on fire. As they were casting on water to quench this fire, the man of God, hearing the tumult, came, and perceiving that there appeared fire in the eyes of the Brethren and not in his, he forthwith bowed his head in prayer, and calling upon those whom he saw deluded with an imaginary fire, he bade them sign their eyes that they might behold the kitchen entire, and not those fantastical flames which the enemy had counterfeited.

CHAPTER XI.

How a boy crushed by the fall of a wall was healed by the servant of God.

Again, when the Brethren were raising the wall a little higher for more convenience, the man of God was at his devotions in his cell, to whom the old enemy appeared in an insulting manner and told him he was going to his Brethren at work; the man of God straightway by a messenger advertized the Brethren thereof saying: "Brethren, have a care of yourselves, for the wicked spirit at this hour is coming to molest you." Scarce had the messenger told his errand when the malignant spirit overthrew the wall that was abuilding, and with the fall thereof crushed a young monk, son to a certain Senator. Here at all of them much grieved and discomforted, not for the loss of the wall but for the harm to their brother, brought the heavy tidings to their venerable Father Benedict, who bid them bring the boy to him, who could not be carried but in a sheet, by reason that not only his body was bruised but also his bones crushed with the fall. Then the man of God willed them to lay him in his cell upon his mat where he used to pray; so causing the Brethren to go out he shut the door, and with more than ordinary devotion fell to his prayers. A wonder to hear, the very same hour he sent him to his work again, whole and sound as ever he was before, to help his Brethren in making up the wall; whereas the old enemy hoped to have had occasion to insult over Benedict for his death.

CHAPTER XII.

Of Monks who had eaten out of their monastery.

Now began the man of God, by the spirit of prophecy, to foretell things to come, and to certify those that were present with him of things that passed far off. It was the custom of the Monastery that the Brethren, sent abroad about any business, should neither eat nor drink anything outside their Cloister. This in the practice of the Rule being carefully observed, one day some Brethren upon occasion went abroad, and were forced to stay later than usual, so they rested and refreshed themselves in the house of a certain devout woman of their acquaintance. Returning late to the Monastery, they asked, as was the custom, the Abbot's blessing, of whom he straightway demanded, saying: "Where dined you?" they answered: "Nowhere." To whom he said: "Why do you lie? Did you not go into such a woman's house? Eat you not there such and such meats? Drank you not so many cups?" When the venerable Father had told them both the woman's lodging, the several sorts of meats, with the number of their draughts, they, in great terror fell down at his feet, and with acknowledgment of all that they had done confessed their fault. But he straightway pardoned them, persuading himself they would never afterwards attempt the like in his absence knowing he was always present with them in spirit.

CHAPTER XIII.

How he reproved the brother of Valentinian the Monk for eating by the way.

Moreover, the brother of Valentinian, the Monk, whom we mentioned in the beginning, was very devout although but a secular; and he used to go to the Monastery from his dwelling once every year and that fasting, that he might partake of the prayers of the servant of God, and see his brother. As he was on his way to the Monastery, another traveller, who carried meat with him, put himself into his company After they had travelled a good while, he said to him: "Come, Brother, let us refresh ourselves, lest we faint by the way." "God forbid!" answered the other, "by no means, Brother, for my custom is always to go to the venerable Father Benedict fasting." At which answer, his fellow-traveller, for the present, said no more; but, when they had gone a little further, he moved him again to ear, but he would not consent because he resolved to keep his fast. So the other was awhile silent, and went forward with him without taking any thing himself. After they had gone a great way, wearied with long travel, in their way they came to a meadow and a spring, with what else might delight them, there to take their repast. Then said his fellow-traveller: "So! Here is water, here is a meadow, here is a pleasant place for us to refresh and rest us awhile, that we may safely make an end of our journey." So, at the third motion, these words pleasing his ear and the place his eye, he was overcome, consented and ate. In the evening he came to the Monastery, where, conducted to the venerable Father Benedict, he craved his prayers, but soon the holy man reproved him for what he had done in the way, saying: "What was it, Brother, the malignant enemy suggested to thee by they fellow traveller? The first time he could not persuade nor yet the second, but the third time he prevailed and obtained his desire." Then the man acknowledging his fault fell at his feet, and began all the more to weep and to be ashamed, by reason that he perceived he had offended, although absent, in the sight of Father Benedict.

PETER.

I discover in the breast of the holy man the spirit of Eliseus, who was present with his disciple though far from him.

CHAPTER XIV.

How he discovered the dissimulation of King Totila.

GREGORY.

You must, Peter, for a little while be silent, that you may know matters far more important. For, in the time of the Goths, their king, informed that the holy man had the gift of prophecy, went towards his Monastery and made some stay a little way off, and gave notice of his coming. To whom answer was made from the Monastery that he might come at his pleasure. The king, being of a treacherous nature, attempted to try whether the man of God had the spirit of prophecy. There was one of his guards called Riggo, upon whom he caused his own buskins to be put and so commanded him taking on him the king's person to go forward to the man of God, three of his chief pages attending upon him, to wit Vulderic, Ruderic and Blindin, to the end they should wait upon him in the presence of the servant of God, that so, by reason of his attendants and purple robes, he might be taken for the king. When the said Riggo, with his brave apparel and attendance, entered the cloister the man of God sat a little distance off, and seeing him come so nigh as he might hear him, he cried to him, saying: "Put off, son, put off that which thou carriest, for it is not thine." Riggo straightway fell to the ground and was much afraid, for having presumed to delude so holy a man; all his followers likewise fell down astonished, and rising, they durst not approach unto him, but returned to their king, and trembling related unto him how soon they were discovered.

CHAPTER XV.

How he prophesied to king Totila and to the Bishop of Canosa.

Then Totila came himself to the man of God, whom as soon as he saw sitting afar off, he durst not come nigh, but fell prostrate to the ground. The holy man twice of three bade him rise, but he durst not get up, then Benedict, the servant of Jesus Christ our Lord, deigned himself to come to the prostrate king, whom, raising from the ground, he rebuked for his deeds, and foretold in a few words all that should befall him saying: "Much evil dost thou do, and much wickedness hast thou done, as least now give over thy iniquity. Into Rome shalt thou enter, thou wilt cross over the sea, nine years shalt thou reign, and die the tenth." At the hearing whereof, the king sore appalled, craved his prayers and departed, but from that time he was less cruel. Not long after he went to Rome, sailed thence to Sicily, and in the tenth year of his reign, by the judgment of Almighty God, lost both crown and life.

Moreover, the Bishop of the Church of Canosa used to come to the servant of God, who much loved him for his virtuous life. He, therefore, conferring with him concerning the coming of king Totila and the taking of the City of Rome, said: "The city doubtless will be destroyed by this king, so that it will never more be inhabited." To whom the man of God replied: "Rome shall never be destroyed by the Pagans, but shall be so shaken by tempests, lightnings and earthquakes that it will decay of itself." The mysteries of which prophecy we now behold as clear as day, for, in this city, we see the walls ruined, houses overturned, churches destroyed by tempestuous winds, and buildings rotten with old age, decay and falling into ruins. Although Honoratus, his disciple, from whose relation I had it, told me heard it not himself from his own mouth but was told it by the Brethren.

CHAPTER XVI.

How venerable Benedict dispossessed a certain clerk from the Devil.

At that time one of the clergy of the church of Aquin was molested with an evil spirit, whom the venerable man, Constantius, Bishop of that Diocese, had sent to divers martyrs' shrines to be cured; but the holy martyrs would not cure him, that the gifts of grace in Benedict might be made manifest. He was therefore brought to the servant of Almighty God, Benedict, who, by pouring forth prayers to our Lord Jesus Christ, presently drove out the enemy. Having cured him, he commanded him, saying: "Go! And hereafter never eat flesh, and presume not to take Holy Orders, for what time soever you shall presume to take Holy Orders, you shall again become a slave to the devil." The Clerk therefore went his way healed, and as present punishments make deep impressions, he carefully for a while observed the man of God's command. But when, after many years, all his seniors were dead and he saw his juniors preferred before him in Holy Orders, he neglected the words of the man of God, as though forgotten through length of time, and took upon him Holy Orders; whereupon, presently, the devil, who before had left him, took power of him, and never ceased to torment him till he severed his soul from his body.

PETER.

This holy man, I perceive, understood the secret decrees of God, in that he knew this Clerk to be delivered to the power of the devil, lest he should presume to receive Holy Orders.

GREGORY.

Why should not he know the secret decrees of Divine Providence, who kept the commandments of God, whence it is written that "he who adhereth to God is one spirit with Him."

PETER.

If he who adhereth to our Lord become one spirit with Him, how comes the same excellent Preacher to say: "Who hath known the mind of the Lord, or who has been His counsellor?" For it seems altogether unlikely that he, who is made one with another, should not know his mind.

GREGORY.

Holy men, so far as they are united with God, are not ignorant of His meaning, for the same Apostle saith; "For what man knoweth the things of a man, but the spirit of a man that is in him? So the things also, that are of God, no man knoweth but the spirit of God." And to shew that he knew things of God, he addeth: "But we have not received the spirit of this world, but the spirit which is of God." And again: "That eye hath not seen, nor ear heard, neither hath it ascended into the heart of man, what things God hath prepared for those that love Him, but to us God hath revealed by His spirit."

PETER.

If then those things which appertained to God were revealed to the said Apostle by the spirit of God, what meaneth he to make this preamble, saying: "O the depth of the riches of the wisdom and knowledge of God; how incomprehensible are His judgments and His ways unsearchable." But as I am saying this, another question arises: for the Prophet David says to our Lord: "With my lips I have uttered all the judgments of Thy mouth." And, whereas, it is less to comprehend or know than to pronounce, what is the reason that St. Paul should affirm the judgments of God to be incomprehensible, while David professeth not only to know them but also to pronounce them with his lips?

GREGORY.

To both these difficulties -- I briefly answered before, when I said: that holy men, as far as they are one with God, are not ignorant of the mind of our Lord, for all such as do devoutly follow the Lord are also by devotion one with God; and yet, in that they are laden with the burden of this corruptible flesh, they are not with God. Therefore, for as much as they are united with God they know His secret judgments, of which likewise they are ignorant for as much as in respect separated from Him: and so they pronounce His judgments incomprehensible which they cannot as yet thoroughly understand. But they who in spirit adhere to Him, in this adhesion know His judgments, either by the sacred words of Scripture, or by hidden revelations, as far as they are capable; these therefore they know and declare, but they are ignorant of those which God concealeth. Whereupon the prophet David when he had said: "In my lips I will pronounce all Thy judgments," as if he had said plainly: "Those judgments I could both know and pronounce which Thou didst tell me, for those which Thou speakest not, without doubt Thou concealest from our knowledge. Thus, the saying of the Prophet agreeth with that of the Apostle, for the judgments of God are both incomprehensible, and yet those which proceed from His mouth are uttered with the lips of men, for being so manifested by God they may be conceived by men, nor can they be concealed.

PETER.

By occasion of the difficulty I propounded, I have obtained a clear solution. But if there remain aught concerning the virtue of this man, I pray you declare it.

CHAPTER XVII.

How he prophecied the destruction of his Monastery.

A certain nobleman, named Theoprobus, was by the admonition of Father Benedict converted, and for the merit of his life was very familiar and intimate with him. He one day entered into the cell of the man of God, found him weeping bitterly; when he had waited a good while and saw he did not give over, (though it was his custom in prayer mildly to weep and not to use any doleful lamentations) he boldly demanded of him the cause of so great grief. To whom the man of God presently replied: "All this Monastery which I have built, with whatsoever I have prepared for my Brethren, are, by the judgment of Almighty God, delivered over to the heathen: and I could scarce obtain to save the lives of those in this place. His words Theoprobus heard, but we see them verified in the destruction of his Monastery by the Longobards. For of late these Lombards, by night, when the Brethren were are rest, entered the Monastery and ransacked all, yet had not the power to lay hand on any man. But Almighty God fulfilled what he had promised to His faithful servant, Benedict, that although he gave their goods into the hands of the Paynims, yet he preserved their lives. In this Benedict did most clearly resemble St. Paul, whose ship with all its goods being lost, yet, for his comfort, he had the lives of all that were in his company bestowed upon him.

CHAPTER XVIII.

How St. Benedict discovered the hiding of a flagon of wine.

Our monk Exhilaratus, whom you know well, on a time was sent by his master with two wooden vessels (which we call flagons) full of wine, to the man of God in his Monastery. He brought one but hid the other in the way, notwithstanding, the man of God, although he was not ignorant of anything done in his absence, received it thankfully, and advised the boy as he was returning back, in this manner: "Take care, son, thou drink not of that flagon which thou hast hid, but turn the mouth of it downward and then thou wilt perceive what is in it." He departed from the holy man much ashamed, and desirous to make further trial of what he had heard, held the flagon downwards, and presently there came forth a snake, at which the boy was sore affrighted and terrified for the evil he had committed.

CHAPTER XIX.

How the man of God reproved a Monk for receiving certain napkins.

Not far distant from the monastery was a certain town in which no small number of people, by the exhortations of Benedict, were converted from the worship of idols to the faith of God. In that place were certain religious women, and the servant of God, Benedict, used to send often some of his Brethren thither to instruct and edify their souls. One day, as his custom was, he appointed one to go; but the Monk who was sent, after his exhortation, by the entreaty of the Nuns, took some small napkins and hid them in his bosom. As soon as he came back, the man of God began very sharply to rebuke him, saying: "How hath iniquity entered thy breast?" The Monk was amazed, and because he had forgotten what he had done, he wondered why he was so reprehended. To whom the holy Father said: "What! Was not I present when thou tookest the napkins of the handmaids of God and didst put them in thy bosom?" Whereupon he presently fell at his feet, and repenting of his folly threw away the napkins which he had hid in his bosom.

CHAPTER XX.

How the man of God understood the proud thought of one of his Monks.

One day as the venerable Father late in the evening was at his repast, it happened that one of his Monks, the son of a lawyer, held the candle to him; and whilst the man of God was eating, he standing in that manner, began by the suggestion of pride to say within himself, "Who is he whom I should wait upon at table, or hold the candle unto with such attendance? Who am I who should serve him?" To whom the man of God presently turning, checked him sharply saying: "Sign thy breast, Brother, what is this you say? Sign thy breast." Then he forthwith called upon the Brethren and willed them to take the candle out of his hand, and bade him for that time to leave his attendance and sit down quietly by him. The Monk being asked afterward of the Brethren concerning his thoughts at that time, told them how he was puffed up with a spirit of pride, and what he spake against the man of God secretly in his own heart. By this it was easily to be perceived that nothing could be kept from the knowledge of venerable Benedict, in whose ears the words of unspoken thoughts resounded.

CHAPTER XXI.

Of two hundred measures of meal found before the man of God's cell.

At another time also in the country of Campania began a great famine, and all people suffered from great scarcity of food, so that all the wheat in Benedict his Monastery was spent, and likewise almost all the bread, so that but five loaves remained for the Brethren's refection. When the venerable Father perceived them sad, he endeavoured by a mild and gentle reproach to reprehend their pusillanimity, and with fair promises to comfort them, saying: "Why is your soul sad for want of bread? To day you are in want but to-morrow you shall have plenty." The next day there were found two hundred sacks of meal before the Monastery gates, by whom God Almighty sent it as yet no man knoweth. Which when the Monks beheld, they gave thanks to God, and by this were taught in their greatest want to hope for plenty.

PETER.

Tell me, I pray you, is it to be thought that this servant of God had continually the spirit of prophecy, when himself pleased, or only at certain times with some discontinuance.

GREGORY.

The spirit of prophecy, Peter, doth not always cast his beams upon the understanding of the Prophets, for as it is written of the Holy Ghost: "He breatheth where He will." So likewise must we conceive, also, when He pleaseth. And, therefore, Nathan being asked by the king if he might build the Temple, first allowed him to do it, and afterwards forbade him. This was the reason that Eliseus knew not the cause why the woman wept but said to his servant who did oppose her: "Let her alone for her soul is in anguish, and the Lord hath concealed it from me and hath not made it known." Thus Almighty God of His great mercy so disposeth in His providence, for the end that by giving the spirit of prophecy sometimes, and at other times withdrawing it, the minds of the Prophets be both elevated above themselves, and also be kept in humility, for by receiving the spirit they may know they are inspired by God, and again they receive it not, they may consider what they are of themselves.

PETER.

It standeth with good reason what you have said. But, I beseech you, prosecute what else you remember of the venerable Father Benedict.

CHAPTER XXII.

How by a vision, he gave order to construct

The Monastery of Terracina.

At another time, he was requested by a certain devout man to send some of his disciples to build a Monastery on his estate near the city of Terracina. To which request he consented, and sent some Monks, appointing an Abbot and Prior over them. As they were setting forward, he promised, saying: "Go, and upon such a day I will come and shew you where to build the Oratory, where the Refectory and lodging for the guests, or what else shall be necessary." So they received his blessing and departed, in hope to see him at the appointed day, for which they prepared all things they thought fit and necessary for their Father and his company. The night before the appointed day the man of God appeared in sleep to him whom he had constituted Abbot and to his Prior, and described to them most exactly how he would have the building ordered. When they awaked, they related to each other what they had seen, yet not altogether relying upon that vision, they expected the man of God according to his promise, but seeing he came not at his appointed time, they returned to him very pensive, saying: "We have expected, Father, your coming, as you promised, but you came not to shew us where and what we should build." To whom he said: "Why, Brethren, why do you say so? Did not I come according to my promise?" And when they said: "When came you?" he replied: "Did I not appear to each of you in your sleep and describe every place? Go, and according to the direction given you in that vision construct the Monastery." Hearing this they were much astonished, and so, returning to the manor, they erected the whole building according to the revelation.

PETER.

I would gladly be informed how and in what manner he could express his mind to them so far off, so they should both hear and understand by an apparition.

GREGORY.

What is the reason, Peter, thou dost so curiously search out the manner how it was done? It is evident that the spirit is of more mobile nature than the body. And we are taught by Scripture how the Prophet was taken up in Judea and set down, with the dinner he carried, in Chaldea, and, after he had refreshed another Prophet with his dinner, found himself again in Judea. If then Habacuc in a moment could corporally go so far and carry his dinner, what wonder if Father Benedict obtained to go in spirit and intimate to the spirits of his Brethren what was necessary; that as the other went corporally to convey corporal food, so he might go in spirit to inform them of things concerning a spiritual life?

PETER.

I confess that by this your discourse you have given full satisfaction to my doubtful mind; but I would gladly know what kind of man he was in his common conversation.

CHAPTER XXIII.

How certain Religious women were absolved

After their death.

GREGORY.

Even his ordinary discourse, Peter, had a certain efficacious virtue, for his heart being elevated in contemplation, he would not allow a word to pass from his mouth in vain. If at any time he spake aught, yet not as one that determined what was best to be done, but by way of threatening, his words had the same force as if he had absolutely decreed it. For, not far from his Monastery, two Nuns of noble race and parentage lived in a place of their own: and a certain Religious man provided them with all things for their exterior. But as in some, nobility of birth causeth baseness in mind, so those, who bear in mind their own greatness do less humble themselves in this world. There aforesaid Nuns had not, as yet, refrained their tongues by a Religious habit, but, by their unadvised speeches, oftentimes provoked to anger the Religious man who had care over them. Wherefore, after he had for a long time endured their contumelious language, he complained to the man of God of the injuries he suffered. Which as soon as he heard he commanded them forthwith, saying: "Have a care of your tongues, for if you do not amend I excommunicate you." Which sentence of excommunication notwithstanding, he did not pronounce but threaten. Yet for all this, they nothing changed in their former conditions. Within a few days after they departed this life, and were buried in the Church. At such time as a Solemn Mass was sung, and the Deacon, as the custom is, cried aloud: "If there be any that communicateth not, let him go forth," then their nurse, who used to make offerings to our Lord for them, saw them rise out of their graves and go forth. This she often observed, that, when the Deacon cried in that manner, they went out, not able to remain in the Church, and, calling to mind what the man of God had said to them whilst they were living, (for he excluded them from communion unless they amended their language and manners) she, with great sorrow, informed the servant of God what she had seen. He presently with his own hands gave the offering saying: "Go and cause this oblation to be offered to our Lord, and they shall be no longer excommunicated." When therefore, this offering was made, and the Deacon, according to custom, cried out that such as did not communicate should go out of the Church, they were not seen to go forth any more. Whereby it was apparent that, whereas they went not forth with the excommunicated, they were admitted by our Lord to communion.

PETER.

It is marvellous strange that this man, although venerable and most holy, as yet living in the mortal body, should be able to release those who were standing at the invisible tribunal.

GREGORY.

And was not he, Peter, yet in this flesh who heard; "Whatsoever thou shalt bind upon earth shall be bound also in Heave, and whatsoever thou shalt loose on earth shall be loosed also in Heaven." Whose place and authority in binding and loosing they possess, who, by faith and virtuous life, obtain the dignity of holy government. And that man, an earthly creature, might receive this power, the Creator of Heaven and earth came down from Heaven to earth and that flesh might judge of spiritual things He became man for the redemption of mankind. For God thus condescending beneath Himself raised our weakness above itself.

PETER.

For the virtue of his miracles your words do yield a very good reason.

CHAPTER XXIV.

Of a boy who was cast out of his grave.

GREGORY.

Upon a certain day, a young Monk of his, who was over-much affected towards his parents, went from the Monastery to their abode without his benediction, and the very same day, as soon as he was come to them he died. The day following his burial they found his body cast up, which they interred the second time, and the next day after it was found in like manner lying above ground as before. Hereupon they ran straight way and fell at the feet of the most mild Father Benedict imploring his aid, to whom the man of God with his own hand gave the communion of the Lord's Body saying: "Go, and lay the Body of the Lord upon his breast and so bury him." This done, the earth kept his body, and never after cast it up. You perceive, Peter, of what merit this man was with our Lord Jesus Christ, sith the very earth cast forth the body of him who had not received the blessing of Benedict.

PETER.

I do plainly perceive it, and am much astonished thereat.

CHAPTER XXV.

Of the Monk, who leaving his Monastery

met a dragon in the way.

One of his Monks of a wandering and inconstant disposition, would by no means abide in the Monastery. Although the man of God had often reproved and admonished him of it, he would in no wise consent to remain in the congregation, and often entreated earnestly to be released. So the venerable Father, overcome with his importunity in anger bade him begone. Scarce was he got out of the Monastery, when he met in the way a dragon who, with open mouth made towards him. Seeing it ready to devour him, he began to quake and tremble, crying out aloud: "Help, help, for this dragon will devour me." The Brethren upon this ran out, yet saw no dragon, but took the panting and afrightened Monk back again to the Monastery, who forthwith promised never to depart and from that time he remained always constant in his promise. He, by the prayers of the holy man, was made to see the dragon ready to devour him, which before he had followed unperceived.

CHAPTER XXVI.

Of the boy cured of the Leprosy.

But I must not pass over in silence what I heard of a very honourable man named Anthony, who affirmed that a servant of his father fell into a leprosy, insomuch that his hair fell off, and his skin was swollen so that he could no longer hide the increase of his disease. Who being sent by the gentleman's father to the man of God, he was by him quickly restored to his former health.

CHAPTER XXVII.

How St. Benedict miraculously procured money

for a poor man to discharge his debt.

Nor will I conceal that which his disciple Peregrine was wont to relate: how, on a certain day, an honest man, constrained by the necessity of a debt, thought his only remedy was to have recourse to the man of God, and acquaint him with his necessity. So he came to the Monastery, where finding the servant of Almighty God, told him how he was extremely urged by his creditor for the payment of twelve shillings. The venerable father answered him that, in very deed, he had not twelve shillings, but yet he comforted his want with good words, saying: "Go, and after two days return hither again for today I have it not to give thee." These two days, as his custom was, he spent in prayer, and, on the third day, when the poor debtor came again, thirteen shillings were found upon a chest of the Monastery that was full of corn. These the man of God caused to be brought to him, and gave them to the distressed man, saying that he might pay twelve, and have one to defray his charges.

But to return to those things which I learned of his disciples of whom I spoke in the beginning of this book, there was a certain man had an adversary who bore him deadly hatred, and so great was his malice that he gave him poison in his drink; which potion, although it procured not his death, yet so altered his colour that his body became all speckled like a leper. This man was brought to the man of God and was quickly restored to his former health; for as soon as he touched him, the diversity of colours vanished from his skin.

CHAPTER XXVIII.

How a bottle was cast down upon the

Stones and not broken.

At such time as the great famine was in Campania, the man of God gave all he had in his Monastery to those in want, insomuch as there was almost nothing left in the cellar save only a little oil in a glass vessel. When one Agapitus, a Subdeacon, came earnestly entreating to have a little oil given him, the man of God (who had resolved to give all upon earth that he might have all in Heaven) commanded this little oil that was left to be given him. The Monk, who was Cellarer, heard his command but was loath to fulfill it. And the holy man a little while after demanded whether he had done what he willed him, and the Monk answered that he had not given it, because if he had given it, there would be nothing left for the Brothers. Hereat, much displeased, the good father bade some other take the glass bottle in which there remained a little oil, and cast it out of the window, to the end that nothing of the fruits of disobedience might remain in the Monastery. This was accordingly done; under the window was a steep fall, full of huge rough stones, upon which the glass fell, yet it remained as whole and entire as if it had not been thrown down, so that neither was the glass broke nor the oil spilt. Then the man of God commanded it to be taken up and given to him that asked it. Then calling the Brothers together, he rebuked the disobedient Monk before them all for his pride and unfaithfulness.

CHAPTER XXIX.

How an empty barrel was filled with oil.

Having ended the Chapter, he and all the Brethren fell to their prayers. In the place where they prayed was an empty oil-barrel close covered. As the holy man continued his prayer, the cover of the said tun began to be heaved up by the oil increasing under it, which ran over the brim of the vessel upon the floor in great abundance. Which so soon as the servant of God, Benedict, beheld, he forthwith ended his prayer, and the oil ceased to run over. Then he admonished the distrustful and disobedient brother to have confidence and learn humility. So the brother thus reprehended was much ashamed, because the venerable Father had by his admonition and by his miracle shewn the power of Almighty God, nor could anyone afterwards doubt of what he promised, since, as it were in a moment, for a glass bottle almost empty, he had restored a tun full of oil.

CHAPTER XXX.

How he delivered a Monk from the devil.

One day as he was going to St. John's Oratory, which stands upon the very top of the mountain, he met the old enemy upon a mule, in the habit and comportment of a physician, carrying a horn and a mortar; who, being demanded whither he went, answered he was going to the monks to minister a potion. So the venerable Father Benedict went forward to the chapel to pray, and, having finished, returned back in great haste, for the wicked spirit found one of the ancient Monks drawing water, and presently he entered into him, threw him on to the ground and tortured him pitifully. As soon as the man of God, returning from prayer, found him thus cruelly tormented, he only gave him a blow on the cheek with his hand, and immediately drave the wicked spirit out of him, so that he durst never after return.

PETER.

I would know whether he obtained these great miracles always by prayer, or did them some times only by the intimation of his will?

GREGORY.

They who are perfectly united with God, when necessity requireth, work miracles both ways, sometimes they do wonders by prayer, sometimes by power. For since St. John saith: "As many as received Him, to them He gave power to become sons of God." What wonder is it if they have the privilege and power to work miracles who are exalted to the dignity of children of God. And that they work miracles in both ways is manifest in St. Peter, who by prayer, raised Tabitha from death, and punished with death Ananias and Sapphira for their falsehood. For we do not read that he prayed when they fell down dead, but only that he rebuked them for their fault committed. It is evident therefore that these things are done sometimes by power, sometimes by petition: since that by reproof he deprived these of their life, and by prayer revived the other.
But now I will produce two other acts of the faithful servant of God, Benedict, in which it shall clearly appear that some things he could do by power received from Heaven, and others by prayer.

CHAPTER XXXI.

How a country man was loosed by only the sight of the man of God.

A certain Goth named Galla was of the impious sect of the Arians, and he, in the time of their king Totila did, with such monstrous cruelty, persecute religious men of the Catholic Church, insomuch that if any cleric or monk came in his sight, he was sure not to escape from his hands alive. This man enraged with an insatiable covetousness of spoil and pillage, lighted one day upon a husbandman whom he tortured with cruel torments. The rustic, overcome with pain, professed that he had committed his goods to the custody of the servant of God, Benedict. This he feigned that he might free himself from torments and prolong his life for some time. Then this Galla gave over tormenting him, and tying his arms together with a strong cord, made him run before his horse to shew him who this Benedict was, that had received his goods. Thus the man went in front, having his arms bound, and brought him to the holy man's Monastery, whom he found sitting alone at the Monastery gate reading. Then the countryman said to Galla, who followed furiously after him: "See! This is Father Benedict whom I told you of." The barbarous ruffian, looking upon him with enraged fury, thought to affright him with his usual threats, and began to cry out with a loud voice, saying: "Rise, rise and deliver up this rustic's goods which thou hast received." At whose voice the man of God suddenly lifted up his eyes from reading, and saw him and also the countryman whom he kept bound: thus, as he cast his eyes upon his arms, in a wonderful manner the cords began to fall off so quickly, that no man could possibly have so soon untied them.

When Galla perceived the man whom he brought bound, so suddenly loosened and at liberty, struck into fear at the sight of so great power, he fell prostrate, and bowing his stiff and cruel neck at the holy man's feet, begged his prayers. But the holy man rose not from his reading but called upon the Brethren to bring him to receive his benediction. When he was brought to him, he exhorted him to leave his barbarous and inhuman cruelty. So, vanquished, he departed, never after presuming to ask anything of the countryman, whom the man of God unloosed not by touching but by casting his eye upon. Thus you see, Peter, as I said, that those who are the true servants of Almighty God, sometimes do work miracles by a commanding power, for he who sitting still abated the fury of that terrible Goth and with his only look unloosed the cords wherewith the innocent man's arms were fast pinioned, sheweth, evidently, by the swiftness of the miracle, that he wrought it by a power received. Now I will also shew you how great and strange a miracle he obtained by prayer.

CHAPTER XXXII.

How he raised a child from the dead.

As he was one day in the field labouring with his Brethren, a certain peasant came to the Monastery, carrying in his arms the dead body of his son, and pitifully lamenting his loss, asked for the holy Father Benedict. When they said that he was in the field, he presently laid down the dead body of his son at the Monastery gate, and, as one distracted with grief, began running to find out the venerable father. At the same time the man of God was coming home with his Brethren from labouring in the field, whom, when the distressed countryman espied, he began to cry out: "Restore me my son, restore me my son." But the man of God amazed at this voice said: "What! Have I taken your son from you?" To whom the man replied: "He is dead, come and raise him." When the servant of God heard this he was much grieved, and said: "Go, Brethren, go! This is not a work for us, but such as were the holy Apostles. Why will you impose burdens upon us which we cannot bear?" Notwithstanding, the man enforced with excessive grief, persisted in his petition, swearing that he would not depart unless he raised his son to life. Then the servant of God enquired, saying: "Where is he?" He answered: "Lo! His body lieth at the Monastery Gate." Whither, when the man of God with his Brethren was come, he knelt down and laid himself on the body of the child; then, raising himself and with his hands held up towards Heaven, he prayed: "O Lord, regard not my sins, but the faith of this man who craveth to have his son restored to life, and restore again to this body the soul which thou hast taken from it." Scarce had he finished these words, but all the body of the boy began to tremble at the re-entry of the soul, so that in the sight of all who were present he was seen with wonderful quaking to pant and breathe. Whom he presently took by the hand and delivered alive and sound to his father.

It seemeth to me, Peter, he had not this miracle actually in his power, which he prostrated himself to obtain by prayer.

PETER.

What you have said is undoubtedly true, because you prove by deeds what was said in words. But I pray, certify me, whether holy men can effect and obtain whatsoever they will or desire?

CHAPTER XXXIII.

Of the miracle wrought by his sister Scholastica.

GREGORY.

Who was ever, Peter, in this life more sublime than St. Paul, who, notwithstanding, three times craved of our Lord to be free from the pricks of the flesh, yet could not obtain it? To this purpose, I must tell you a passage concerning the venerable Father Benedict, that there was something he desired and was not able to accomplish.

His sister Scholastica, who was consecrated to God from her very childhood, used to come once a year to see him; unto whom the man of God was wont to go to a house not far from the gate, within the possession of the Monastery. Thither she came one day according to her custom, and her venerable brother likewise with his disciples: where, after they had spent the whole day in the praise of God and pious discourses, the night drawing on, they took their refection together. As they were yet sitting at table, and protracting the time with holy conference, the religious woman, his sister, entreated him saying: "I beseech you, leave me not this night, that we may talk until morning of the joys of the heavenly life." To whom he answered: "What is this you say, sister? By no means can I stay out of my Monastery." At this time the sky was serene, and not a cloud was to be seen in the air. The holy woman, therefore, hearing her brother's refusal, clasped her hands together upon the table, and bowing her head upon them she prayed to Almighty God. As she raised up her head from the table, there began such vehement lightning and thunder, with such abundance of rain, that neither venerable Benedict nor his Brethren were able to put foot out of doors. For the holy woman when she leaned her head upon her hands, poured forth a flood of tears upon the table by which she changed the fair weather into foul and rainy. For, immediately after her prayers, followed the inundation, and the two did so concur that, as she lifted up her head, the crack of thunder was heard, so that in one and the same instant she lifted up her head and brought down the rain. Then the man of God perceiving that, by reason of thunder and lightening with continual showers of rain, he could not possibly return to his monastery, was sad and began to complain, saying: "God Almighty forgive you, sister, what is this you have done?" To whom she made answer: "I prayed you to stay and you would not hear me; I prayed to Almighty God and He heard me! Now, therefore, if you can, go forth to the Monastery and leave me." But he not able to go forth, was forced to stay against his will.

Thus it fell out that they spent the night in watching, and received full content in spiritual discourse of heavenly matters. By this it appears, as I said before, that he desired something which he could not obtain; for if we consider the mind of the venerable man, he would, without doubt, have had the fair weather to continue in which he set out. But, contrary to what he willed, he found a miracle worked by the courage of a woman in the strength of Almighty God. And no wonder if at that time a woman were more powerful than he, considering she had long desired to see her brother. For according to the saying of St. John: "God is charity," and with good reason she was more powerful who loved more.

PETER.

I confess that I am wonderfully pleased with that which you tell me.

CHAPTER XXXIV.

In what manner St. Benedict saw the soul of his sister go forth from her body.

GREGORY.

The next day, the venerable woman returned to her Cloister and the man of God to his Monastery. When, behold, three days after, while standing in his cell, he saw the soul of his sister depart out of her body, and, in the form of a dove, ascend and enter into the celestial mansions. Who rejoicing much to see her great glory, gave thanks to God Almighty in hymns and praises, and announced her death to the Brethren. Whom he forthwith sent to bring her body to the Monastery, and caused it to be buried in the same tomb that he had prepared for himself. By means of which it fell out, that as their minds were always one in God, so also their bodies were not separated in their burial.

CHAPTER XXXV.

How the whole world was repesented before his

Eyes: and the soul of Germanus, Bishop of Capua.

Another time, Servandus, Deacon and Abbot of that Monastery which was
built by Liberius, sometime a senator, in the Campania, used often to
visit him, for being also illuminated with grace and heavenly doctrine,
he repaired divers times to the Monastery that they might mutually
communicate one to another, and, at least with sighs and longing
desires, taste of that sweet food of the celestial country whose
perfect fruition they were not as yet permitted to enjoy. When it was
time to go to rest, venerable Benedict went up to the top of the tower
in the lower part of which Servandus the Deacon had his lodging, and
from which there was an open passage to ascend to the higher. Over
against the said tower was a large building in which the disciples of
both reposed. While as yet the Monks were at rest, the man of God,
Benedict, being diligent in watching, rose up before the night office
and stood at the window making his prayer to Almighty God about
midnight, when suddenly, looking forth, he saw a light glancing from
above, so bright and resplendent that it not only dispersed the
darkness of the night, but shined more clear than the day itself. Upon
this sight a marvellous strange thing followed, for, as he afterwards
related, the whole world, compacted as it were together, was
represented to his eyes in one ray of light. As the venerable Father
had his eyes fixed upon this glorious lustre, he beheld the soul of
Germanus, Bishop of Capua, carried by angels to Heaven in a fiery
globe. Then, for the testimony of so great a miracle, with a loud voice
he called upon Servandus the Deacon, twice or thrice by his name,
who, troubled at such an unusual crying out of the man of God, came
up, looked forth, and saw a little stream of light then disappearing, and
wondered greatly at this miracle. Whereupon the man of God told him
in order all that he had seen, and sent presently to Theoprobus, a
Religious man in the town of Cassino, ordering him to go the same
night to Capua, and learn what had happened to Germanus the Bishop.
It fell out so, that he who was sent found the most reverend Bishop
Germanus dead, and on enquiring more exactly, he learned that his departure was the very same moment in which the man of God had seen

him ascend.

PETER.

A wonderful thing and much to be admired, but, whereas you said that the whole world, as it were, under one sunbeam, was represented to his sight, as I never experienced the like, so I cannot imagine how or in what manner this was possible that the whole world should be seen of any one man.

GREGORY.

Assure yourself, Peter, of that which I speak: that in a soul that beholdeth the Creator, all creatures appear but narrow; for, should we partake never so little of the light of the Creator, whatsoever is created would seem very little; because the soul is enlarged by this Beatific vision, and so dilated in the Divine perfections, that it far transcends the world and itself also. The soul thus rapt in the light of God is in her interior lifted up, and enabled above itself, and while thus elevated it contemplates itself, and it easily comprehendeth how little that is which before it was not able to conceive. So the blessed man who saw the globe of fire with the Angels returning to Heaven could not possibly have beheld those things but only in the light of God. What wonder then if he saw the world at one view who was in mind exalted above the world? But whereas I said that the whole world compacted as it were together was represented before his eyes, it is not meant that heaven and earth were straitened by contraction, but that the mind of the beholder was dilated, which, rapt in the sight of God might, without difficulty, see all that is under God. Therefore, in that light which appeared to his outward eyes, the inward light which was in his soul ravished the mind of the beholder with higher things, and shewed how mean are all inferior things.

PETER.

I perceive that it was to my profit that I understood you not before, for my slowness has been the occasion of so long and profitable a discourse. But, since you have clearly explained these things to me, I beseech you continue your former narration.

CHAPTER XXXVI.

How he wrote a Rule for Monks.

I would willingly, Peter, relate many things concerning this venerable Father, but some of purpose I omit, because I hasten to speak of the acts of others. Only this I would not have you to be ignorant of, that the man of God, among so many miracles wherewith he shined to the world, was also eminent for his doctrine, for he wrote a Rule for Monks both excellent for discretion and eloquent in style. Of whose life and conversation if any wish to know further, he may in the institution of that Rule understand all his manner of life and discipline, for the holy man could not possibly teach otherwise than he lived.

CHAPTER XXXVII.

How he prophetically foretold his death to his Brethren.

The same year in which he departed out of this life, he foretold the day of his most holy death to some of his disciples who conversed with him, and to others who were far off; giving strict charge to those who were present to keep in silence what they had heard, and declaring to the absent by what sign they should know when his soul departed out of his body. Six days before his departure he caused his grave to be opened, and immediately after he fell into a fever, by the violence whereof his strength began to wax faint, and the infirmity daily increasing, the sixth day he caused his disciples to carry him into the Oratory, where he did arm himself for his going forth by receiving the Body and Blood of the Lord; then, supporting his weak limbs by the hands of his disciples, he stood up, his hands lifted towards Heaven, and with words of prayer at last breathed forth his soul. The same day two of his Brethren, the one living in the Monastery and the other in a place far remote, had a revelation in one and the self-same manner. For they beheld a way, spread with garments and shining with innumerable lamps, stretching directly eastwards from his cell up to Heaven; a man of venerable aspect stood above and asked them whose way that was. But they professing they knew not, he said to them: "This is the way by which the beloved of the Lord, Benedict, ascended." Thus the disciples who were present knew of the death of the holy man, and so also those who were absent understood it by the sign foretold them. He was buried in the Oratory of St. John the Baptist which he himself had built upon the ruins of Apollo's altar.

CHAPTER XXXVIII.

How a mad woman was cured in his cave.

In the cave also in which he formerly lived in Subiaco, even to this day, miracles are wrought upon such as repair thither with true faith. For very lately happened that which I now relate. A certain woman bereft of reason, and altogether distracted in her senses, roamed over mountains and valleys, through woods and fields by day and night, never resting, except when forced from weariness to lie down. One day, as she raged thus madly up and down, she lighted upon the cave of blessed Benedict, and by chance entered and remained there. The next morning she came out as sound and perfect in her senses as if she had never been out of them, and from that time remained all her life in the health which she had there recovered.

PETER.

What should be the reason that we experience, even in the patronage of martyrs, that they do not bestow so great favours by their bodies as by their relics: yea, and do greater miracles where themselves be not?

GREGORY.

Where the bodies of holy martyrs lie, no doubt, Peter, but there they are able to shew many miracles, as they do; for to such as have recourse unto them, with pure mind, they shew many marvellous favours. But forasmuch as weak souls might doubt whether they be present to hear them or no in those places where their bodies be not, it is necessary to shew more miracles where weak souls may doubt of their presence. For they whose minds are fixed in God have so much the greater merit of faith, that though their bodies lie not there, yet they be there present to hear our prayers. Wherefore Truth Itself to increase the faith of His disciples said: "If I go not away the Paraclete will not come unto you." For whereas it is certain, that the Holy Ghost, the Comforter, always proceedeth from the Father and the Son: why doth the Son say that He will go from them that the Paraclete may come, who never departeth from the Son? But because the Disciples behold-ing our Lord in the flesh, did desire always to behold Him with their corporeal eyes, it was rightly said unto them: "Unless I go away the

Paraclete will not come." As if He had said plainly: If I withdraw not My bodily presence, I do not shew you the love of the Spirit: and, unless you cease to see Me carnally, you will never learn to love spiritually.

PETER.

What you say pleaseth me.

GREGORY.

Let us now for a while cease our discourse, that by silence we may be the better enabled to prosecute the miracles of other saints.

THE END.

CHRONOLOGY
OF THE
LIFE OF THE MOST HOLY PATRIARCH
SAINT BENEDICT

(from Haften's Disgnis. Monast.)

"His memory shall not depart away; and his Name shall be in request from generation to generation." (Ecclus. 39)

(The figures in parenthesis denote the age of St. Benedict.)

YEAR.

480. (--) St. Benedict and his twin-sister St. Scholastica are born in Nursia, a town in the south of Italy: their Father, Anicius Eupropius: their Mother, Abundantia.

487. (7.) St; Benedict is sent to Rome to study, his nurse Cyrilla accompanies him.

493. (13.) God, calling him to higher things, and the dangers of the world prompting him to leave it, he quits Rome to seek salvation and perfection in solitude. On their way in a little village, 30 miles from Rome, he works a miracle to console Cyrilla.

494. (14.) He leaves Cyrilla and goes alone to Subiaco, a mountainous district, 40 miles distant from Rome: meets a holy Hermit named Romanus, from whom he asks and receives the Religious Habit: then going into a little Cave amidst the rocks, dwells there in union with his God in prayer, unknown to all, excepting St. Romanus who brought him food.

497. (17.) On the Easter Sunday of this year, a Priest receives a command from God to visit this Cave, and honour the youthful hermit.

Some neighbouring Shepherds discover the Saint.

He gains the noble victory over the spirit of impurity and placing the lily of his Chastity amidst thorns and nettles, he secures it against every temptation for the remainder of his life.

509. (29.) His sanctity becoming noised abroad many men leave the world, and put themselves under his spiritual guidance.

510. (30.) After frequent refusals he, at last, yields to the request of the Monks of Vico-Varro, who besought him to become their Abbot. As he had foretold them they grew angry at his corrections: they seek to poison him: he returns to his dear solitude of Subiaco.

St. Maurus is born.

511. (31.) During the next 19 years St. Benedict builds 12 monasteries on the Subiaco mountains.

515. (35.) St Placid is born.

522. (42.) Sts. Maurus and Placid are brought to Subiaco by their Parents, and receive from St. Benedict the Monastic Habit.

523. (43.) St. Maurus in obedience to St. Benedict walks on the waters of the lake, into which St. Placid had fallen, and saves him from being drowned.

529. (49.) St. Benedict leaves Subiaco, and goes to Mount Cassino (about 50 miles south of Subiaco).

530. (50.) He begins to build the Monastery of Mount Cassino.

536. (56.) He sends St. Placid into Sicily.

St. Benedict has the mysterious vision, in which God grants him the sight of the whole world, brought together in one ray of the sun.

537. (57.) St. Placid begins the Monastery at Messina in Sicily: he finishes it in 4 years.

539. (59.) During a famine St. Benedict distributes to the poor all the corn of the Monastery: on the following day he receives from Heaven, in return, 200 bushels of flour.

In hatred of Disobedience and out of love for Charity he works the miracle of the glass oil-jar.

Whilst he is at prayer with some of his Brethren, an empty vessel which was in the room is miraculously filled with oil, even to over-flowing.

541. (61.) St. Placid is martyred (probably in this year).

543. (63.) King Totila the Barbarian visits St. Benedict: receives his paternal reproach and prophecy.

On the 10th of January, St. Benedict sends St. Maurus into France.

On the 6th of February he has the last conference with his sister St. Scholastica.

On the 10th of February, he sees the soul of his Sister, St. Scholastica, ascending to heaven under the form of a Dove.

On the 16th of March, knowing that the hour of his Death is near he orders his grave to be opened.

On the 21st of March at 3 o'clock in the morning, standing in the chapel of his Monastery of Mount Cassino, supported by his Religious, he dies, in the 63rd year of his age.

THE RULE
OF OUR
MOST HOLY FATHER
SAINT BENEDICT.

Pax multa diligentibus legem tuam.
Mark a monk,
Disciple of the Holy Father Benedict.

While the blind crowd at idol shrines profane devotions paid,
Believing that by mortal hands immortal gods were made,
This fane with altars ruinous by them was whilom built,
Who offered to the impure Jove a sacrifice of guilt;
But holy Benedict, by God called from the desert lone,
Made pure this port, the statues broke, threw down the sculptur'd
stone.

A temple for the living God this idol fane is now:
Let not the faithful soul delay to pay his pious vow;
But hither haste, spite of rough ways; his recompense shall be
That he the heavens opened wide with eye of faith may see.
With hard and toilsome labour 'tis that great things are attained:
Within the narrow path alone the blessed life is gained.

While hither coming penitent bow'd down with load of sin,
I felt its weight was gone from me, I felt at peace within;
And I believe in bliss above I too shall have my share,
If thou for Marcus, Benedict, wilt breathe an earnest prayer.

The foolish people once had called this place a citadel
And dedicated, for their gods of marble there to dwell;
But had they wished to find true words with which to stamp the same,
Tartarean Chaos blank, confused, had been its rightful name.

Hither they wandered, blinded fools, unceasing vows to pay
To the death-dealing thundering Jove, acknowledging his sway.
The hall's high summit, I suppose, he once had struck in vain,
Giving the name of citadel to this now sacred fane.

Against it now shall not prevail gates of eternal Hell:
That which the stronghold was of Death is now Life's citadel.
From here is stormed the golden gate of the bright starry heaven
While the bless'd crowd sing angel strains to angel voices given.

From here, O Hermit thou dost speak to God the Thunderer true
On mountain heights leading thy quire, the faithful chosen few.
When from a mountain far away to this mount thou didst come
Christ wast thy guide, thy path, whilst thou the desert drear didst
roam.

He angels sent to keep thy feet at every cross-way
Lest from the rightful destin'd path thy faltering steps should stray.
He had foretold to thee, just man, alone in desert land,
Avoid these spots, another friend to guide thee is at hand.

Now thou art taken home to him, the mountain's lurid dye
Takes colour from the lowering clouds which hide its top from view.
The caves drip down with copious tears, the barren grottoes mourn,
The beasts their denizens lament--thou hast left all forlorn.

Thee too the lakes and brooks have wept with deep and unfeign'd
grief.
The wood unkempt hath shed for thee each rent and withered leaf.
Fables I speak not when I tell that, following thee anear,
To bear thee faithful company three ravens did appear.

The peoples seek thee out, where thou hast found thy place of rest,
Where thou await'st the holy night, eve of the pious feast.
Like orphans destitute they mourn with hoarse and bitter plaint
Bereft of thy sweet fellowship, thou gentle, perfect Saint.

When thou wert hither brought, behold! The rocks and thorns divide,
And wonder-working fountains spring from the earth's parched side.
Surely the mount of Christ, is Lord o'er all the mountains round;
And yet beneath thy feet it placed its top--twice-hallow'd ground.

For thee with head submiss it makes all its rough places plain
That thou, O holy Saint of Christ, should'st herald forth His reign.
That they who seek thee, Benedict, should not grow faint and tire,
Its gentle slope spreads out for those who upward do aspire.

Tis meet that unto thee the mount itself this honour bring,
Since with thy healing presence thou dost winter turn to spring.
Thou dost lay out its places dry with gardens fair to view;
Thou coverest its sterile rocks with flowers of every hue.

The crags amazed bring forth their crops and harvests not their own,
The greenwood trees bend down with fruits where once was arid stone.
Thus thou dost water hearts of men with healthful streams of prayer
Bidding their vain and barren acts the fruit of grace to bear.

So now, I pray thee, turn the thorns which rend thy Marcus' breast
To fruits unfading of good works, earnest of endless rest.

THE PROLOGUE OF OUR
MOST HOLY FATHER SAINT BENEDICT
TO HIS RULE

Hearken, my son, to the precepts of thy Master, and incline the ear of thy heart willingly to hear, and effectually to accomplish, the admonition of thy living Father, that by the labour of obedience thou mayest return to Him, from Whom thou didst depart by the sloth of disobedience. To thee therefore is my speech now directed, who, renouncing thy own will, dost take upon thee the strong and bright armour of obedience, to fight under the Lord Christ our true King.

First of all whatever good work thou dost begin, beg of Him with most earnest prayer to perfect; that He Who hath now vouchsafed to reckon us in the number of His children, may not be saddened by our evil deeds. For we must at all times so serve Him with the goods He hath bestowed upon us, that He may not either as an angry Father disinherit us His children, or as a dread Lord, exasperated by our offences, deliver us up to perpetual punishment as wicked servants, who would not follow Him to glory.

Let us therefore arise, the Scripture stirring us up and saying, "It is now the hour for us to rise from sleep", [1] and our eyes being opened to the deifying light, let us with wondering ears attend to the admonition with the Divine Voice daily addresseth to us, saying: "Today if you shall hear His voice, harden not your hearts". [2] And again: "He that hath ears, let him hear what the Spirit saith to the Churches." [3] And what saith He? "Come, ye children, and hearken unto Me: I will teach you the fear of the Lord." [4] "Run while ye have the light of life, that the darkness of death overtake ye not." [5]

And our Lord seeking His labourer among the multitude to whom He here speaketh, saith again: "Who is the man that will have life, and desireth to see good days?" [6] If thou, hearing this, dost answer: "I am he": God saith unto thee: "If thou wilt have true and everlasting life, refrain thy tongue from evil, and thy lips, that they speak no guile. Decline from evil, and do good; seek after peace and pursue it." [7] And when you have done this: My eyes shall be upon you, and My ears shall be open to your prayers. And before you can call upon Me, I will say: "Behold I am present." [8] What, dearest brethren, can be sweeter, than this voice of the Lord, inviting us? Behold how in His loving Kindness He showeth unto us the way of life! Our loins therefore being girt with faith and the observance of good works, and our feet shod with the guidance of the Gospel of peace, let us walk in His ways, that we may deserve to see in His kingdom Him Who has called us. [9]

If we desire to dwell in the tabernacle of this kingdom, it can only be by running the way of good works, whereby alone it can be reached. But let us ask our Lord with the Prophet saying to Him: "Lord, who shall dwell in Thy tabernacle, or who shall rest on Thy holy hill?" [10] After this question, Brethren, let us hear our Lord answering and showing us the way to His tabernacle, saying: "He that walketh without spot and worketh justice. He that speaketh truth in his heart, that hath not forged guile with his tongue. He that hath not forged guile with his tongue. He that hath not done evil to his neighbour and hath not received reproach against him." [11]

He that rejecting out of his mind the malignant devil with his suggestions, hath brought them all to nought, and taking his thoughts while they are still young, hath dashed them against the rock Christ. [12] All they who fearing the Lord, take not pride in their good observance, but knowing that all the good they have, or can do, proceedeth not from themselves, but from the Lord, magnify Him, thus working in them, and say with the Prophet: "Not to us O Lord, not to us, but to Thy Name give glory." [13] Thus the Apostle Paul imputed not anything of his preaching to himself, saying: "By the grace of God I am what I am." [14] And again he saith: "He that glorieth, let him glory in the Lord." [15]

Hence also our Lord saith in the Gospel: "He that heareth these My words and doth them,--I will liken him to a wise man that hath built his house upon a rock. The floods came, the winds blew, and beat against that house, and it fell not; because it was founded upon a rock." [16] Our Lord fulfilling these things, daily waiteth for us to answer by our deeds, these His holy admonitions. Therefore the days of our life are prolonged for the amendment of our evil deeds, according to those words of the Apostle: "Knowest thou not that the patience of God leadeth thee to repentance?" [17] For our loving Lord saith: "I will not the death of the sinner, but that he be converted and live."[18]

70

Having therefore, my Brethren, enquired of our Lord who shall be the dweller in this tabernacle, we have heard the precept to the one dwelling, and if we fulfil the functions of this habitation we shall become heirs of the kingdom of heaven. Therefore our hearts and bodies must be prepared to fight under the holy obedience of His commands, and we must beg our Lord to supply that, by the assistance of His grace, which our nature is unable to perform. And if flying the pains of hell we will to attain to everlasting life, we must, while yet time serves, and we live in this flesh, perform all these things by the light of faith, and haste to do that now which will be expedient for us for ever hereafter.

We are therefore now about to institute a school of the service of God; in which we hope nothing will be ordained rigorous or burdensome. But if in some things we proceed with a little severity, sound reason so advising, for the amendment of vices or preserving of charity; do not straightway for fear thereof, flee from the way of salvation which is always strait and difficult in the beginning. [19] But in process of time and growth of faith, when the heart has once been enlarged, the way of God's commandments is run with unspeakable sweetness of love; so that, never departing from His teaching, but persevering in the Monastery in His doctrine until death, we share now by patience in the sufferings of Christ, that we may deserve afterwards to be partakers of His kingdom. [20]

[1] Rom. xiii. 1

[2] Ps. xciv. 8.

[3] Apoc. ii. 7.

[4] Ps. xxxiii. 12.

[5] John. xii. 35.

[6] Ps. xxxiii. 13

[7] Ibid. 14, 15.

[8] Isai. lxv. 24.

[9] Ephes. vi. 14, 15.

[10] Ps. xiv. 4.

[11] Ps. xiv. 2, 3.

[12] Ps. cxxxvi. 9.

[13] Ps. cxiii. 1.

[14] I. Cor. xv. 10.

[15] II. Cor. x. 47.

[16] Matth. vii. 24, seq.

[17] Rom. ii. 4.

[18] Ezech. xviii. 23.

[19] Matth. vii. 13.

[20] II Cor. i. 7.

CHAPTER I.

Of the several kinds of Monks.

It is well known that there are four kinds of Monks. The first are Cenobites, that is Monastics, living under a Rule or Abbot. The second are Anchorites or Hermits, who, not in the first fervour of conversion, but after long probation in the monastic life, have learnt to fight against the devil, and taught by the encouragement of others, are now able by God's assistance to strive hand to hand against the flesh and evil thoughts, and so go forth well prepared, from the army of the Brotherhood, to the single combat of the wilderness. The third and worst kind of Monks are the Sarabiaites, who have never been tried under any Rule, nor by the experience of a master, as gold is tried in the furnace, but being soft as lead, and by their works still cleaving to the world, are known by their tonsure to lie to God.

These in twos or threes, or perhaps singly, and without a shepherd, are shut up, not in our Lord's sheepfolds, but in their own: the pleasure of their desires is to them a law; and whatever they like or make choice of, they will have to be holy, but what they like not, that they consider unlawful.

The fourth kind of Monks are called "Gyrovagi," or wanderers, who travel about all their lives through divers provinces, and stay for two or three days as guests, first in one monastery, then in another; they are always roving, and never settled, giving themselves up altogether to their own pleasures and to the enticements of gluttony, and are in all things worse that the Sarabites. Of their miserable way of life it is better to be silent than to speak. Therefore leaving these, let us, by God's assistance, set down a Rule for Cenobites, or Conventuals, who are the most steadfast class of Monks.

\

CHAPTER II.

What kind of man the Abbot ought to be.

An Abbot who is worthy to have charge of a Monastery ought always to remember what he is called, and in his actions show forth the character of Ancient. For in the Monastery he is considered to represent the person of Christ, seeing that he is called by His name, as the Apostle saith: "Ye have received the spirit of the adoption of children, in which we cry, Abba, Father." [21] Therefore the Abbot ought not (God forbid) to teach, ordain, or command but what is conformable to the commands of our Lord: but let his commands and doctrine be mingled in the minds of his disciples with the leaven of diving justice.

Let the Abbot always be mindful that, in the dreadful judgment of God, he must give an account both of his doctrine and of the obedience of his disciples, and let the Abbot know that any lack of profit which the Master of the family shall find in his sheep, will be laid to the shepherd's fault. But if he have bestowed all diligence on his unquiet and disobedient flock, and employed the utmost care to cure their corrupt manners, he shall then be acquitted in the judgment of the Lord, and may say with the Prophet: "I have not hidden thy justice in my heart, I have told thy truth and thy salvation, [22] but they contemned and despised me." [23] And then finally, death shall be inflicted as a just punishment upon the disobedient sheep.

When, therefore, anyone receives the name of Abbot, he ought to govern his disciples with a twofold doctrine; that is, he ought first to show them all virtue and sanctity, more by deeds than by words: hence, to such as are intelligent, he may declare the commandments of God by words; but to the hard-hearted, and to those of the ruder sort, he must make the divine precepts manifest by his actions. In the next place, let him show by his own deeds, that they ought not to do anything which he has taught them to be unfitting, lest, having preached well to others, "he himself become a castaway," [24] and God say unto him thus sinning: "Why dost thou declare My justices, and take My testament in thy mouth? Thou hast hated discipline, and cast My speeches behind thee, [25] And,--"Thou, who didst see the mote in thy brother's eye, hast thou not seen the beam that is in thine own?" [26]

Let him make no distinction of persons in the Monastery. Let not one be loved more than another, except he be found to surpass the rest in good works and in obedience. Let not one of noble parentage, on coming to Religion, be put before him who is of servile extraction, except there be some other reasonable cause for it. If, upon just consideration, the Abbot shall think there is such a just cause, let him put him in any rank he shall please, but otherwise, let every one keep his own place; because "whether bondman or freeman, we are all one in Christ" [27] , and bear an equal burthen of servitude under one Lord: "for with God there is no accepting of persons." [28] On one condition only are we preferred by Him, and that is, if in good works and in humility we are found better than others. Therefore let the Abbot bear equal love to all; and let all be subject to the same discipline, according to their deserts.

For the Abbot ought always, in his doctrine, to observe that apostolic form wherein it is said; "Reprove, entreat, rebuke." [29] That is to say, he ought, as occasions require, to temper fair speeches with threats: let him show the severity of a master and the loving affection of a father: those who are undisciplined and restless he must reprove sternly, but with such as are obedient, mild and patient, he should deal by entreaty, exhorting them to go forward in virtue. But the stubborn and negligent we charge him to severely reprove and chastise.

Let him not shut his eyes to the sins of offenders, but, as soon as they show themselves, use all possible endeavours utterly to root them out, remembering the fate of Heli, the Priest of Silo. [30] With the more virtuous and intelligent, let him for the first or second time use words of admonition; but the stubborn, the hard-hearted, the proud and the disobedient, even in the very beginning of their sin, let him chastise with stripes and bodily punishment, knowing that it is written: "The fool is not corrected with words." [31] And again: "Strike thy son with the rod, and thou shalt deliver his soul from death." [32]

The Abbot ought always to remember what he is, and what he is called, and know that unto whom more is entrusted, from him more is exacted, and let him consider how difficult and hard a task he hath undertaken, to govern souls, and to accommodate himself to the humours of many, some of whom must be led by fair speeches, others by sharp reprehensions, and others by persuasion. Therefore let him so adapt himself to the character and intelligence of each one, that he may not only suffer no loss in the flock committed to him, but may even rejoice in the increase and profit of his virtuous flock.

Above all things, let him take heed not to slight or make little account of the souls committed to his keeping, and have more care for fleeting, worldly things than for them; but let him always consider that he hath undertaken the government of souls for which he shall also have to give an account. And that he may not complain for want of temporal means, let him remember that it is written: "Seek ye first the kingdom of God and His justice, and all things shall be given ye." [33] And again: "Nothing is wanting to such as fear Him." [34]

Let him know that the man who undertakes the government of souls must prepare himself to give an account of them. And how great soever the number of brethren may, let him know certain that at the day of judgment he will have to give to the Lord an account for all their souls as well as for his own. Thus, by fearing the examination which the shepherd must undergo for the flock committed to his charge, he is made solicitous on other men's account as well as careful on his own; and while reclaiming them by his admonitions, he is himself freed from all defects.

[21] Rom. viii. 15.

[22] Ps. xxxix. ii.

[23] Is. I. 2.

[24] I Cor. ix, 27.

[25] Ps. xlix. 16, 17.

[26] Matth. vii. 3.

[27] I. Cor. xii. 13; Rom. ii. ii..

[28] Ephes. vi. 9.

[29] II Tim. iv. 2.

[30] I. Reg. ii, 12 seq..

[31] Prov. xxiii. 13.

[32] Ibid. 14.

[33] Matth. vi. 33.

[34] Ps. xxxiii. 19.

CHAPTER III.

Of calling the brethren to council.

As often as any weighty matters have to be debated in the monastery, let the Abbot call together all the Brethren, and himself declare what is the point under deliberation. Having heard their counsel, let him prudently weigh it with himself, and then do what he shall judge most expedient. The reason why we ordain that all be called to Council, is because the Lord often revealeth to the younger what is best. And let the Brethren give their advice with all subjection and humility, and presume not stiffly to defend their own opinion, but rather leave it to the discretion of the Abbot; and what he shall think more expedient, to that, let them all submit; for, as it becometh the disciples to obey their master, so doth it behove the master to dispose all things with forethought and justice.

In all things, therefore, let all follow the Rule as their master, and from it let no man rashly swerve. Let no one in the monastery follow his own will. Neither let anyone presume, within or without the monastery, to contend insolently with his Abbot. If he do so, let him be subjected to regular discipline. Let the Abbot, however, do all things with the fear of God, and in observance of the Rule, knowing that he shall undoubtedly give an account of all his judgments to God, the most just Judge. If any matters of less moment have to be done for the benefit of the monastery, let him take counsel with the seniors only, as it is written: "Do all things with counsel, and thou shalt not afterwards repent thee of it." [35]

[35] Eccli. xxxii. 24..

CHAPTER IV.

What are the instruments of good works.

First of all, to love the Lord God with all our heart, with all our soul, with all our strength. [36]

2. Then our neighbour as ourself. [37]

3. Then not to kill. [38]

4. Not to commit adultery. [39]

5. Not to steal. [40]

6. Not to covet. [41]

7. Not to bear false witness. [42]

8. To honour all men. [43]

9. Not to do to another what we would not have done to ourselves. [44]

10. To deny ourselves, in order to follow Christ. [45]

11. To chastise the body. [46]

12. Not seek after delights. [47]

13. To love fasting. [48]

14. To relieve the poor. [49]

15. To clothe the naked. [50]

16. To visit the sick. [51]

17. To bury the dead. [52]

18. To help those that are in tribulation. [53]

19. To comfort the sad. [54]

20. To withdraw ourselves from worldly ways. [55]

21. To prefer nothing to the love of Christ. [56]

22. Not to give way to anger. [57]

23. Not to harbour revenge in our mind. [58]

24. Not to foster guile or deceit in our heart. [59]

25. Not to make a feigned peace. [60]

26. Not to forsake charity. [61]

27. Not to swear at all, lest we forswear ourselves. [62]

28. To speak the truth with heart and mouth. [63]

29. Not to render evil for evil. [64]

30. Not to do any injury; yea, and patiently to bear an injury done to us. [65]

31. To love our enemies. [66]

32. Not to speak ill of such as speak ill of us, but rather to speak well of them. [67]

33. To suffer persecution for justice sake. [68]

34. Not to be proud. [69]

35. Not given to wine. [70]

36. Not a great eater. [71]

37. Not drowsy. [72]

38. Not slothful. [73]

39. Not a murmurer. [74]

40. Not a detractor. [75]

41. To put our trust in God. [76]

42. When we see any good in ourselves let us attribute it to God and not to ourselves. [77]

43. But let us always know that evil is done by ourselves, therefore let us attribute it to ourselves. [78]

44. To fear the day of judgment. [79]

45. To be afraid of hell. [80]

46. To desire life everlasting with spiritual thirst. [81]

47. To have death always before our eyes. [82]

48. To observe at every hour the actions of our life. [83]

49. To know for certain that God beholdeth us in every place. [84]

50. To dash at once against Christ the evil thoughts that rise in the mind. [85]

51. To reveal all such to our spiritual Father. [86]

52. To keep our mouth from evil and wicked words. [87]

53. Not to love much talking. [88]

54. Not to speak vain words, nor such as move to laughter. [89]

55. Not to love much and boisterous laughter. [90]

56. Willingly to hear holy readings. [91]

57. To pray often devoutly. [92]

58. With tears and sighs, daily to confess our past evils to God in prayer and to amend them for the time to come. [93]

59. Not to fulfil the desires of the flesh, and to hate self-will. [94]

60. To obey in all things the commands of the Abbot, though he himself (which God forbid) should do otherwise, being mindful of that precept of our Lord: "What they say, do ye; but what they do, do ye not." [95]

61. Not to desire to be called holy, before we be so, and first to be holy, that we may truly be called so. [96]

62. Daily to fulfil in deeds the commandments of God. [97]

63. To love chastity. [98]

64. To hate no man. [99]

65. To flee envy and emulation. [100]

66. Not to love contention. [101]

67. To flee Haughtiness. [102]

68. To reverence the Elders. [103]

69. To love inferiors. [104]

70. For Christ's sake to pray for our enemies. [105]

71. To make peace with adversaries before the setting of the sun. [106]

72. Never to despair of God's mercy. [107]

Behold these are the tools or instruments of our spiritual profession: if we constantly employ them day and night, and have them signed with approval in the day of judgment, that reward shall be given us by our Lord as a recompense "Which eye hath not seen, nor ear heard, nor hath it entered into the heart of man to conceive what God hath prepared for those that love Him." [108] The workshop where all these things are to be done is the cloister of the monastery, and steadfast abiding in the Congregation.

[36] Deut. vi. 5.

[37] Luc. x. 27.

[38] Luc. xviii. 20.

[39] Matth. xix. 18.

[40] Exod. xx. 15.

[41] Deut. vi. 21.

[42] Marc. x. 19.

[43] I. Petr. ii. 17.

[44] Tob. iv. 16.

[45] Luc. ix. 23.

[46] I Cor. ix. 27.

[47] II. Petr. ii. 13.

[48] Joel i. 14; ii, 12, 15.

[49] Tob. iv. 7..

[50] Is. lviii. 7.

[51] Matth. xxv. 36.

[52] Tob. i. 21, ii. 4, 7-9.

[53] Is. i. 17.

[54] I. Thes. v. 14.

[55] Jac. i. 27.

[56] Matth. x. 37, 38.

[57] Matth. v. 22.

[58] Ephes. iv. 26.

[59] Ps. xiv. 3.

[60] Rom. xii. 18.

[61] I. Petr. iv. 8.

[62] Matth. v. 33-37.

[63] Ps. xiv. 3.

[64] I. Thes. v. 15.

[65] I. Cor. vi. 7.

[66] Luc. vi. 27-35.

[67] I. Petr. iii. 9.

[68] Matth. v. 10.

[69] Tob. iv. 14.

[70] I. Tim. iii. 3.

[71] Eccli. xxxi. 17.

[72] Prov. xx. 13.

[73] Rom. xii. 11.

[74] I Cor. x. 10.

[75] Sap. i. 11.

[76] Ps. lxxii. 28.

[77] I Cor. iv. 7.

[78] Ose. xii. 9.

[79] Job. xxxi. 14.

[80] Matth. x. 28.

[81] Phil. i. 23.

[82] Matth. xxiv. 42 et seq..

[83] Deut. iv. 9.

[84] Prov. v. 21.

[85] Ps. cxxxvi. 9.

[86] Eccli. viii. ii.

[87] Ps. xxxiii. 13, 14.

[88] Prov. x. 19.

[89] Matth. xii. 35.

[90] Eccli. xxi. 23.

[91] Luc. xi. 28.

[92] Col. iv. 2.

[93] Ps. vi. 7.

[94] Gal. v. 16.

[95] Eccli. xviii. 30.

[96] Matth. xxiii. 3.

[97] Matth. vi. i.

[98] Eccli. vi. 37.

[99] I. Tim. v. 22.

[100] Levit. xix. 17.

[101] Jacob. iii. 14, 16.

[102] II. Tim. ii. 24.

[103] Ps. cxxx. 1.

[104] Levit. xix. 32.

[105] I Tim. v. i..

[106] Matth. v. 44.

[107] Ephes. iv. 26.

[108] Ps. li. 10.

CHAPTER V.

Of the obedience of disciples.

The first degree of humility is obedience without delay. This beseemeth those who, either on account of the holy servitude they have professed, through fear of hell or for the glory of life everlasting, count nothing more dear to them than Christ. These, presently, as soon as anything is commanded them by the Superior, make no delay in doing it, just as if the command had come from God. Of such, our Lord saith: "At the hearing of the ear he hath obeyed me." [109] And to teachers He saith: "He that heareth you, heareth me." [110] Therefore, such as these, leaving immediately everything, and forsaking their own will, leave unfinished what they were about, and with the speedy foot of obedience follow by deeds the voice of him who commands. And thus, as it were in one and the same moment the command of the master and the perfect work of the disciple in the speed of the fear of God, go both jointly together, and are quickly effected by those who ardently desire to advance in the way of eternal life. These take the narrow way, of which the Lord saith: "Narrow is the way which leadeth to life." [111] They live not according to their own will, nor follow their own desires and pleasures, but, abiding in monasteries, walk according to the command and direction of another, and will to have an Abbot over them. Without doubt these fulfil that saying of our Lord: "I came not to do my own will, but the will of Him Who sent me." [112]

This obedience will then be acceptable to God and pleasing to men, if what is commanded be not done fearfully, slowly, coldly, or with murmuring, or an answer showing unwillingness; because the obedience which is given to superiors is given to God, Who hath said: "He that heareth you, heareth Me." [113] Hence it ought to be done by the disciples with a good will, because God "loveth a cheerful giver" [114] If the disciple obey with ill-will, and murmur, not only in words, but also in heart, although he fulfil what is commanded him, it will not be acceptable to God, Who considereth the heart of the murmurer. For such a work he shall not have any reward, but rather incurreth the penalty of murmurers, unless he amend and make satisfaction.

[109] I Cor. ii. 9.

[110] Ps. xvii. 45.

[111] Matth. vii. 14.

[112] John. v. 30.

[113] Luc. x. 16.

[114] II Cor. ix. 7.

CHAPTER VI.

Of Silence.

Let us act in accordance with that saying of the Prophet; "I have said: I will keep my ways, that I offend not with my tongue. I have been watchful over my mouth: I held my peace and humbled myself, and was silent from speaking even good things." [115] If therefore, according to this saying of the Prophet we are at times to abstain, for silence sake, even from good talk, how much more ought we to refrain from evil words, on account of the penalty of sin. Therefore, because of the importance of silence, let leave to speak be seldom given, even to perfect disciples, although their words be of good and holy matters, tending unto edification; because it is written: "In much speaking, thou shalt not escape sin." [116] And in another place: "Death and life are in the hands of the tongue." [117] For it befitteth a master to speak and teach; and it beseemeth a disciple to hold his peace and listen.

If, therefore, anything must be asked of the Prior, let it be done with all fitting humility and the subjection of reverence. But as for buffoonery, idle words, or such as move to laughter, we utterly condemn and exclude them in all places, nor do we allow a disciple to open his mouth to five them utterance.

[115] Ps. xxxviii. 2. 3.

[116] Prov. x. 19.

[117] Prov. xviii. 21.

CHAPTER VII.

Of Humility.

The Holy Scripture crieth to us, Brethren, saying: "Everyone who exalteth himself shall be humbled, and he who humbleth himself shall be exalted." [118] By these words it declares to us, that all exaltation is a kind of pride, which the Prophet showeth must carefully be avoided when he says: "Lord, my heart is nor exalted, neither are my eyes lifted up: neither have I walked in great things, nor in wonders above myself." But why? "If I did not think humbly, by exalted my soul: as a child weaned from his mother, so wilt Thou reward my soul." [119]

Wherefore, Brethren, if we would attain to the highest summit of humility, and speedily reach that heavenly exaltation, which is won through the lowliness of this present life; by our ascending actions a ladder must be set up, such as appeared in sleep to Jacob, whereon he saw Angels descending and ascending.

That descent and ascent signifieth nothing else, but that we descend by exalting, and ascend by humbling ourselves.

The latter thus erected, is our life here in this world, which through humility of heart is lifted up by our Lord to heaven. The sides of this ladder we understand to be our body and soul, in which the Divine Vocation hath placed divers degree of humility and discipline, which we must ascend.

The first degree, then, of humility is that a man always have the fear of God before his eyes, and altogether fly forgetfulness. Moreover to be mindful of all that God hath commanded, and remember that such as contemn God fall into hell for their sins, and that everlasting life is prepared for such as fear Him. And keeping himself every moment from all sin and vice, of thought, word, eyes, hands, feet, and self will, let him thus hasten to cut off the desires of the flesh.

Let him think that he is always beheld from Heaven by God; that all his actions, wheresoever he may be, lie open to the eye of God, and are at every hour presented before Him by His Angels. The Prophet declareth this, when, in these words, he saith that God is always present to out thoughts: "God searcheth the heart and reins." [120] And again: "The Lord knoweth the thoughts of men, that they are vain." [121] He alto saith: "Thou hast understood my thoughts afar off," [122] and: "The thought of man shall confess to Thee." [123] In order therefore that the humble Brother may be careful to avoid evil thoughts, let him always say in his heart: "Then shall I be without spot before Him, if I shall keep me from my iniquity." [124]

The Scripture also forbiddeth us to do our own will, saying: "Leave thy own will and desire." [125] And again: "We beg of God in prayer, that His Will may be done in us." [126]

With good reason, therefore, are we taught to beware of doing our own will, when we keep in mind that which the Scripture saith: "There are ways which to men seem right, and end whereof plungeth even into the deep pit of hell." [127] And again when we fear that which is said of the negligent: "They are corrupted, and made abominable in their pleasures." [128] But in the desires of the flesh, we ought to believe God to be always present with us, according to that saying of the Prophet, speaking to the Lord: "O Lord, all my desire is before Thee." [129]

Let us then take heed of evil desires, because death sitteth close to the entrance of delight. Wherefore the Scripture commandeth us: "Follow not thy concupiscences." [130] If then the eyes of the Lord behold both good and bad; if He ever looketh down from heaven upon the sons of men to see who is understanding or seeking God: if our works are told to Him day and night by our Angels; we must always take heed, Brethren, lest, as the Prophet saith in the Psalm, "God behold us some time declining to evil, and become unprofitable;" [131] and though He spare us for the present, because He is merciful, and expecteth our conversion, He may yet say to us hereafter: "These things thou hast done, and I have held My peace." [132]

The second degree of humility is, if anyone, not wedded to his own will, seeks not to satisfy his desires, but carries out that saying of our Lord: "I came not to do My own Will, but the Will of Him Who sent Me." [133] The scripture likewise saith: "Self-will engendereth punishment, and necessity purchaseth a crown."

The third degree of humility is, that a man submit himself for the love of God, with all obedience to his superior, imitating thereby our Lord, of Whom the Apostle saith: "He was made obedient even unto death." [134]

The fourth degree of humility is, that if, in obedience, things that are hard, contrary, and even unjust be done to him, he embrace them with a quiet conscience, and in suffering them, grow not weary, nor give over, since the Scripture saith: "He only that persevereth to the end shall be saved." [135] And again, "Let thy heart be comforted, and expect the Lord." [136] And showing that the faithful man ought to bear all things for our Lord, be they never so contrary, it saith in the person of the sufferers: "For Thee we suffer death all the day long; we are esteemed as sheep for the slaughter." [137] And being assured by hope of a reward from God's Hands they go on rejoicing and saying: "But in all things we overcome by the help of Him Who hath loved us." [138]

Likewise in another place the Scripture saith: "Thou hast proved us, O Lord, Thou hast tried us, as silver is tried, with fire. Thou hast brought us into the snare; Thou hast laid tribulation upon our backs." [139] And to shew that we ought to be under a Prior it goes on to say: "Thou hast placed men over our heads." [140] Moreover, in order to fulfil the precepts of the Lord by patience in adversities and injuries: "When struck on one cheek, they offer the other; to him who taketh away their coat, they leave their cloak also; and being constrained to carry a burthen one mile, they go two." [141] With Paul the Apostle they suffer false Brethren and persecutions, and bless those who speak ill of them. [142]

The fifth degree of humility is to manifest to the Abbot, by humble confession, all the evil thoughts of his heart, and the secret faults committed by him. The Scripture exhorteth us thereunto, saying: "Reveal thy way to the Lord, and hope in Him." [143] And again: "Confess thy way to the Lord because He is good, because His mercy endureth for ever." [144] Furthermore the Prophet saith: "I have made known unto Thee mine offence, and mine injustices I have not hidden. I have said, I will declare openly against myself mine injustices to the Lord; and Thou hast pardoned the wickedness of my heart." [145]

The sixth degree of humility is, if a Monk be content with all that is meanest and poorest, and in everything enjoined him, think himself an evil and worthless servant, saying with the Prophet: "I have been brought to nothing, and knew it not. I have become as a beast before Thee, and I am always with Thee." [146]

The seventh degree of humility is, not only to pronounce with his tongue, but also in his very heart to believe himself to be the most abject, and inferior to all; and humbling himself, to say with the Prophet: "I am a worm and no man, the reproach of men and the outcast of the people. [147] I have been exalted, humbled, and confounded." [148] And again: "It is good for me that Thou hast humbled me, that I may learn thy commandments." [149]

The eighth degree of humility is, that a Monk do nothing but what the common rule of the Monastery, or the examples of his seniors, exhort him to do.

The ninth degree of humility is, for a Monk to refrain his tongue from speaking, and be silent till a question be asked him, remembering the saying of the Scripture: "In many words thou shalt not avoid sin," [150] and "a talkative man shall not be directed upon the earth." [151]

The tenth degree of humility is, not to be easily moved and prompt to laugh, for it is written: "The fool exalteth his voice to laughter." [152]

The eleventh degree of humility is that when a Monk speaketh, he do so, gently and without laughter; humbly, with gravity or few words, and discreetly; and be not clamorous in his voice; for it is written: "A wise man is known by few words." [153]

The twelfth degree of humility is, that a Monk not only have humility in his heart, but show it also in his exterior, to all the behold him; so that whether he be at the work of God, in the Oratory, the monastery, the garden, on the way, in the field or wherever he may be, whether he sit, walk, or stand, let him always, with head bent down, and eyes fixed upon the earth, think of himself guilty for his sins, and about to be presented before the dreadful judgment of God, ever saying to himself with the Publican in the Gospel: "Lord, I a sinner am not worthy to lift up mine eyes to heaven." [154] And again with the Prophet: "I am bowed down and humbled on every side." [155]

Thus, when all these degrees of humility have been ascended, the Monk will presently come to that love of God which is perfect and casteth our fear; to that love, whereby everything, which at the beginning he observed through fear, he shall now begin to do by custom, without any labour, and as it were naturally; not now through fear of hell, but for the love of Christ, our of a good custom, and a delight in virtue. All this our Lord will vouchsafe to work by the Holy Ghost in His servant, now that he is cleansed from defects and sins.

[118] Luc. liv. 11.

[119] Ps. cxxx. 1. 2.

[120] Ps. vii. 10..

[121] Ps. xciii. 11.

[122] Ps. cxxxviii. 3.

[123] Ps. lxxv. 11.

[124] Ps. xvii. 24.

[125] Eccli. xviii. 30.

[126] Matth. vi. 10.

[127] Prov. xvi. 25.

[128] Ps. lii. 24.

[129] Ps. xxxvi. 10.

[130] Eccli. xviii. 30.

[131] Ps. lii. 4.

[132] Ps. xlix. 21.

[133] Joan. vi. 38.

[134] Phil. ii. 8.

[135] Matth. xxiv. 13.

[136] Ps. xxvi. 14..

[137] Ps. xliii. 22.

[138] Rom. viii. 37.

[139] Ps. lxv. 10. 11.

[140] Ibid. 12.

[141] Matth. v. 39-41.

[142] II. Cor. xi. 26.

[143] Ps. xxxvi. 5.

[144] Ps. cv. 1.

[145] Ps. xxxi. 5.

[146] Ps. lxxii. 22. 23.

[147] Ps. xxi. 7.

[148] Ps. lxxxvii. 16..

[149] Ps. cxviii. 71.

[150] Prov. x, 10.

[151] Ps. cxviii. 12.

[152] Eccli. xxi. 23.

[153] Eccles. x.

[154] Luc. xviii. 13.

[155] Ps. cxviii. 107.

CHAPTER VIII.

Of the Divine Office at night-time.

In winter, that is from the first of November till Easter, they shall rise at that time which reasonable calculation shall indicate as the eighth hour of the night, in order that having rested till a little after midnight, they may rise refreshed. As for the time that remains after Matins, let it be employed in study, by those Brethren who are somewhat behind-hand in the psalter and lessons. But from Easter till the first of November, let the hour for Matins be so arranged, that after a short interval during which they may go forth for the necessities of nature, Lauds may presently follow about the break of day.

CHAPTER IX.

How many psalms are to be said in the night-hours.

In winter, having first said the verse, "O God incline unto mine aid, O Lord make haste to help me," [156] the words, "O Lord open my lips, and my mouth shall declare Thy praise," [157] are next to be repeated three times After this the third Psalm is said, with a "Glory be to the Father," at the end. Then the ninety-fourth Psalm is to be recited or sung with an antiphon. Let hymn follow next, and then six psalms with antiphons. These being said, and a versicle added, let the Abbot give a blessing, and then, all being seated, let three lessons be read by the Brethren in turns, from the book lying on the lectern. After every lesson, let a responsory be sung. Let two of them be without a "Gloria," but after the third let it be added by the Cantor, and as soon as he has begun it, let all rise from their seats our of honour and reverence to the Holy Trinity.

Let the divinely inspired books, both of the Old and New Testament, be read at Matins, together with the expositions made upon them by the most famous, orthodox, and Catholic Fathers. After these three lessons and their responsories, let six other psalms follow, to be sung with an Alleluia. Then let a lesson from the Apostle be said by heart, and after that a verse and the supplication of the Litanies, that is, "Kyrie eleison." And thus let the Matins or Night-watches be brought to an end.

[156] Ps. lxix. 2.

[157] Ps. l. 17.

CHAPTER X.

How Matins, or Night-office, is to be celebrated in Summer.

From Easter till the first of November, let the same number of psalms be recited, as we have before appointed; but let not the lessons be read, because of the shortness of the nights. Instead of these three lessons, let one out of the Old Testament be said by heart, followed by a short responsory, and let all the rest be performed as we have before arranged, so that without counting the third, and the ninety-fourth psalms, there be never fewer than twelve psalms said at Matins.

CHAPTER XI.

How Matins, or Night-office, is to be celebrated on Sundays.

On Sunday, let them rise more seasonably for Matins, and therein observe the following order. When six psalms and the versicle have been sung, as we before arranged, let all sit down in a becoming and orderly manner, and let four lessons with the responsories be read from the book; to the forth responsory only, let the Cantor add a "Gloria," at the beginning of which all shall rise out of reverence. After these lessons, let six more psalms follow in order, with their antiphons and versicle as before. Then let four other lessons with their responsories be read in the same way as the former. Next, let three canticles be said our of the Prophets, such as the Abbot shall appoint; these must be sung with "Alleluia."

When the versicle has been said, and the Abbot has given his blessing, let four other lessons out of the New Testament be read, in the same order as before.

After the fourth responsory, let the Abbot begin the Hymn "Te Deum laudamus," and this being said, let him read a lesson from the Gospel, with reverential fear while all stand. At the end of this let all answer "Amen", and then let the Abbot go on with the Hymn: "Te decet alus." Then, after the giving of the blessing, let Lauds begin. This order is always to be observed in singing Matins on Sundays, both in summer and in Winter, except perchance (which God forbid) they rise late, for then the lessons or responsories must be somewhat shortened. But let good care be taken that this do not happen; and if it do, let him, by whose negligence it comes to pass, make satisfaction for it in the Oratory.

CHAPTER XII.

How the solemnity of Lauds is to be performed.

For Sunday's Lauds, first, let the sixtieth Psalm be said plainly, without an antiphon; after which, say the fiftieth with an "Alleluia;" then the hundred-and-seventeenth, and the sixty-second; then the "Blessings," [158] and "Praises" [159] , one lesson out of the Apocalypse said by heart, a responsory, a hymn, a versicle with a canticle out of the Gospel, and the Litanies, and so conclude.

[158] The Cant. Of the Three Children. "the Benedicite."

[159] Pss. cxlviii. cxlix, cl. of which almost every verse begins by the word "Laudate," were called "Laudes".

CHAPTER XIII.

How Lauds are to celebrated on ferial or week days.

On ferial days, let Lauds be celebrated thus: Let the sixty-sixth Psalm be said as on Sunday, plainly and without an antiphon, and also somewhat more slowly, in order that all may be in their places for the fiftieth, which must be said with an antiphon. After which, let two other psalms be said according to custom; that is, on Monday, the fifth and thirty-fifth. On Tuesday, the forty-second and fifty-sixth. On Wednesday, the sixty-third and sixty-fourth. On Thursday, the eighty-seventy and eighty-ninth. On Friday, the seventy-fifth and ninety-first. On Saturday, the hundred-and-forty-second and the Canticle of Deuteronomy, which must be divided into two "Glorias." But on other days, let the Canticle our of the Prophets be said, each on its own day, according to the practice of the Roman Church. After these, let the Praises follow; then a lesson from the Apostles, to be said by heart, a responsory, hymn, and versicle, a Canticle out of the Gospel, the Litanies, and so conclude.

Let not the celebration of Lauds, or Evensong, ever terminate, unless at the end, the Lord's prayer be said by the Prior, in the hearing of all, because of the thorns of scandal which are wont to arise; that the Brethren, being reminded by the covenant of this prayer, in which they say: "Forgive us our trespasses as we forgive them the trespass against us", may purge themselves from these faults. But in celebrating the other hours let the last part only be said aloud, that all may answer: "But deliver us from evil."

CHAPTER XIV.

In what manner the Office of Matins is to be celebrated on the Feast days of Saints.

On Saints' days, and upon all solemnities, let the same order be observed as upon Sundays, only that psalms, antiphons, and lessons be said, proper to the day itself. Their method, however, shall remain the same as before determined.

CHAPTER XV.

At what seasons "Alleluia" must be said.

From the holy feast of Easter until Whitsuntide, let "Alleluia" be said without intermission, as well with the psalms, as with the responsories. From Whitsuntide till the beginning of Lent, let it be said at all the Night-Offices, with the six last psalms only. But on every Sunday out of Lent, let the Canticles, Lauds, Prime, Tierce, Sext and None, be said with "Alleluia." Let Even-song, however, be said with antiphons. Let the responsories never be said with "Alleluia," except from Easter till Whitsuntide.

CHAPTER XVI.

In what manner the Work of God is to be done in the day time.

"Seven times a day", saith the Prophet. "have I sung praises unto Thee." [160] This sacred number of seven shall be accomplished by us if at the times of Lauds, Prime, Tierce, Sext, None, Even-song, and Complin, we perform the duties of our service. It was of these hours the Prophet said: "

Seven times in the day I have sung praise to Thee." For of the Night-watches, the same Prophet says: "At midnight I did arise to confess to Thee." [161] At these times therefore, let us give praise to our Creator for the judgments of His justice; that is at Lauds, Prime, Tierce, Sext, None, Even-song, and Complin; and in the night let us rise to confess unto Him.

[160] Ps. cxviii. 164.

[161] Ibid. 62.

CHAPTER XVII.

How many psalms are to be said during the aforesaid hours.

We have already arranged the order of the Office for the Nocturns, or Lauds; let us now dispose of the Hours that follow. At Prime, let three psalms be said separately, and not under one "Gloria." Presently after the verse: "O God incline unto mine aid," let the hymn of the same Hour follow, before the psalms be begun. At the end of the psalms, let there be recited one lesson, a versicle, and "Kyrie eleison," and let that Hour conclude with a collect. Tierce, Sext, and None, are to be recited in the same way; that is, the prayer, versicle, and hymns of these same Hours, three psalms, then a lesson, versicle, and "Kyrie eleison", and let the Hour conclude with a collect. If the community be great, let the Hours be sung with antiphons; if, however, it be small, let them be only recited. Let Even-Song be said with four psalms and antiphons; after these let a less on be recited, then a responsory, the hymn, versicle, and canticle, our of the Gospel--the Litany, the Lord's Prayer, and a collect to conclude. For Complin, let three psalms be recited straight on without antiphons. After these, the hymn for that Hour, the lesson, versicle, "Kyrie eleison", and blessing, and so let the Hour terminate.

CHAPTER XVIII.

In what order the psalms are to be said.

In the day Hours, let the verse "O God incline unto mine aid, O Lord make haste to help me," always be said first, and after it a "Gloria." Then the hymn proper to each Hour. On Sundays, at Prime, there must be said four divisions of the hundred-and-eighteenth Psalm. At the rest of the Hours, to wit, at Tierce, Sext and None, let there be said three divisions of the same hundred-and-eighteenth Psalm. But on Monday at Prime, let three psalms be said, that is, the first, second, and sixth. In the same way at Prime, let three psalms be said in order every day, till Sunday, as far as the nineteenth Psalm: yet in such a way that the ninth and seventeenth Psalms be divided into two "Glorias." Thus it will fall out that on Sunday at Matins we shall always begin from the twentieth Psalm.

At Tierce, Sext, and None, on Mondays, let the remaining nine divisions of the hundred-and-eighteenth Psalm be said, three at a time, during these same Hours. On two days therefore, to wit, Sunday and Monday, the hundred-and-eighteenth Psalm being gone through, let the psalms at Tierce, Sext, and None, on Tuesdays be sung in order, three at a time, from the hundred-and nineteenth to the hundred-and-twentyseventh, that is nine psalms. These psalms are always to be repeated at the same Hours for the rest of the week till Sunday; a uniform order also of the hymns, lessons, and versicles, being sung every day observed, so that every Sunday they may being with the hundred-and-eighteenth Psalm.

Even song is to be sung every day with four psalms, which are to begin from the hundred-and-ninth, and go on to the hundred-and-forty-seventh, such only being excepted as are set apart for other Hours, that is, from the hundred-and-seventeenth, to the hundred-and-twenty-seventh, and from the hundred-and-thirty-third to the hundred-and-forty-second; all the rest are to be said in Even-song. And because there fall three psalms short, those of the aforesaid number that are longer, must be divided, that is, the hundred-and-thirty-eighth, the hundred-and-forty third, and the hundred-and-forty-fourth. But let the hundred-and-sixteenth, because it is short, be joined with the hundred-and-fifteenth.

The order, therefore, of the psalms for Evensong being set down, let other matters such as lessons, responsories, hymns, versicles, and canticles, be arranged as before. At Complin let the same psalms be repeated every day: the is, the fourth, ninetieth, and the hundred-and-thirty-third. The order of the day office being thus disposed of, let all the psalms which remain be equally portioned out into seven Night-Watches, or Matins, and such of them as are too long, divided into two. Let twelve psalms be appointed for every night. If this arrangement and distribution of the psalms displease anyone, let him, if he think good, order them otherwise, provided however he take care, that every week the whole psalter of one hundred-and-fifty psalms be sung; and that on Sunday at Matins, they begin it again; for Monks show themselves to be over negligent and indevout, who do not in the course of a week sing over the psalter with the usual canticles, since we read that out holy Fathers courageously performed in one day, what, God grant, that we who are negligent and tepid, may perform in a whole week.

CHAPTER XIX.

Of the order and discipline of singing.

We believe that the Divine Presence is everywhere, and that the eyes of the Lord behold both the good and the bad, in all places; but we believe this especially and without any doubt, when we assist at the Word of God. Let us, therefore, always be mindful of what the Prophet saith: "Serve ye the Lord in fear." [162] And again: "Sing ye His praises with understanding." [163] And: "In the sight of Angels I will sing praise unto Thee." [164] Therefore, let us consider in what manner it behoveth us to be in the sight of God and of the Angels, and so let us sing in choir, that mind and voice may accord together.

[162] Ps. ii. 11.

[163] Ps. xliv. 8.

[164] Ps. cxxxviii. 1.

CHAPTER XX.

Of reverence at prayer.

If, when we wish to make some suggestion to the powerful, we presume not to speak to them except with humility and reverence; with how much greater reason ought we to present our supplications in all humility and purity of devotion, to the Lord God of all things? And let us bear in mind, that we shall be heard, not for our many words, but for our purity of heart, and our penitential tears. [165] Our prayer, therefore, ought to be short and pure, unless perchance it be prolonged by the inspiration of Diving Grace. Yet, let all prayer made in common be short, and when the sign has been given by the Prior, let all rise together.

[165] Matth. vi. 7.

CHAPTER XXI.

Of the Deans of the Monastery.

If the Community be large, let men of good repute and saintly lives be chosen from among the Brethren and appointed Deans, to be careful over their Deaneries in all things, according to the command of God, and the precepts of their Abbot. Let such men be chosen for Deans as the Abbot may safely rely upon to share his burthens; and let them not be chosen by order, but according to the merit of their lives and learning. And if perchance any of them, being puffed up with pride, shall be found blameworthy, and being thrice rebuked, shall show no sign of amendment, let him be put out of office, and a more worthy man substituted in his place. Concerning the Provost, we make the same ordinance.

CHAPTER XXII.

How the Monks are to sleep.

Let them sleep, each in separate beds, and receive, according to the appointment of the Abbot, bedclothes befitting their condition. If it be possible, let them all sleep in one place; but if the number do not allow of this, let them repose by tens or twenties in one place with their Seniors who have care of them. And let a candle burn constantly in that same cell until morning. Let them sleep clothed, and girt with girdles or cords, but let them not have knives by their sides while they sleep, lest perchance they be hurt therewith; and thus let the Monks always be ready, that when the sign is given they may rise speedily, and hasten, each one, to come before his Brother to the Work of God, but yet with all gravity and modesty.

Let not the younger Brethren have beds in a place apart by themselves, but separated among the Elders. And when they rise to the work of God, let them gently encourage one another, because of the excuses of those who are sluggish.

CHAPTER XXIII.

Of excommunication for offences.

If any Brother be found stubborn, disobedient, proud, murmuring, or in any way gainsaying the holy Rule, or contemning the orders of his Elders, let him, in accordance with the precept of the Lord, be once or twice secretly admonished by them. If he amend not, let him be reprehended publicly before all. But if in spite of all this he do not correct himself, let his be subjected to excommunication, provided he understand the nature of the punishment. But if he remain obstinate, let him undergo corporal chastisement.

CHAPTER XXIV.

What the manner of excommunication ought to be.

The measure of excommunication or punishment should be meted our according to the quality of the faults; but the estimation of their gravity shall depend upon the judgment of the Abbot. If any Brother be found guilty of small faults, let him be deprived of eating at table with the rest. The manner of his punishment shall be as follows: In the Oratory he shall not intone a psalm or antiphon, nor read a lesson, until he has made satisfaction. He shall take his portion of food after the Brethren have taken theirs, in such quantity, and at such time as the Abbot shall deem fit. If, for example, the Brethren take their refection at the sixth hour, let him take his at the ninth; if the Brethren take theirs at the ninth, let him take his in the evening, until by due satisfaction he obtain pardon.

CHAPTER XXV.

Of more grievous faults.

Let that Brother who is guilty of more grievous faults be denied both the table and the Oratory. Let none of the Brethren discourse with him not keep him company. Let him be alone at the work enjoined him, continuing in penance and sorrow, knowing that terrible sentence of the Apostle, who saith, "That such a one is delivered over to Satan for the destruction of the flesh, that his spirit may be saved in the day of our Lord." [166] Let him take his portion of food alone, in such measure and at such time as the Abbot shall think fit: let not anyone bless him as he passes by, not the food that is given to him.

[166] I. Cor. v. 5.

CHAPTER XXVI.

Of those who keep company with the excommunicated without the command of the Abbot.

If any Brother shall presume, without the command of the Abbot, to join himself in any way to the excommunicated Brother, or to talk with him, or send him a message, let him incur the same penalty of excommunication.

CHAPTER XXVII.

How the Abbot ought to care for the excommunicated.

Let the Abbot have a special care of the offending Brethren, for, "They that are well need not the physician, but they that are sick." [167] He ought, therefore, like a wise physician, to use every means in their regard, and covertly send them as comforters, some elderly and discreet Brothers to console, as it were secretly, the wavering one, and win him to make humble satisfaction. Let them comfort him, that he be not swallowed up by overmuch sorrow, but as the Apostle saith: "Let charity be confirmed towards him, and let all pray for him." [168]

The Abbot ought especially to have care, and with all prudence and industry, to see that he lose none of the sheep committed to his charge. Let him know that he hath undertaken the care of sick souls, and not a tyrannical authority over such as are well. Let him fear the threat of the Prophet, by whom God saith; "What ye saw to be fat, that ye took to yourselves, and what was diseased, that ye threw away." [169] Let him imitate the loving kindness of the "Good Shepherd," Who "leaving ninety-nine sheep in the mountains, went to seek one that had gone astray, on whose infirmity He took such compassion, that He vouchsafed to lay it on His own sacred shoulder, and thus carry it back to the flock." [170]

[167] Matth. ix. 12.

[168] I Cor. ii. 8.
[169] Ezech. xxxiv. 3.
[170] Luc. xv. 4.

CHAPTER XXVIII.

Of those who, being often corrected, do not amend.

If any Brother after being corrected, or even excommunicated for any fault, doth not amend, let a sharper correction be administered to him: that is to say, let him be punished with stripes. But if for all that he do not correct himself, or being puffed up with pride (which God forbid) shall also defend his doings; then let the Abbot act like a wise physician, and after applying the fomentations and ointments of exhortation, the medicines of the Divine Scriptures, and last of all the punishment of excommunication and of scourging; then, if he find that his labours have no effect,--let him add what is more that all this,--his own prayer, and the prayer of the Brethren for him, that the Lord, Who can do all things, would vouchsafe to work a cure upon the infirm Brother. If he be not healed and corrected by this means, then let the Abbot use the sword of separation, according to that saying of the Apostle: "Put away the evil one from among you." [171] And again: "If the faithless one depart, let him depart," [172] lest one diseased sheep should infect the whole flock.

[171] I. Cor. v. 13.

[172] I. Cor. vii. 15.

CHAPTER XXIX.

Whether the Brethren who leave the monastery ought to be received again.

If that Brother, who through his own fault leaveth, or is cast out of the Monastery, be willing to return, he shall first promise to amend the fault for which he went forth; then let him be received into the lowest rank, that by this, his humility may be tried. If he go out again, let him be received back till the third time. But after this let him know that all entrance will be denied him.

CHAPTER XXX.

How children are to be corrected.

Every age and understanding ought to have a measure of government suitable to it. As often therefore as children, or those under age, commit faults, and are incapable of understanding the greatness of the punishment of excommunication, let them be punished by rigorous fasting, or sharp stripes, that so they may be corrected.

CHAPTER XXXI.

What kind of man the Cellarer of the monastery ought to be.

Let there be chosen out of the Community as Cellarer of the Monastery, a man who is wise, ripe in manners, and sober; not a great eater, not haughty, nor hasty, nor insulting; not slow, nor wasteful, but fearing God, and acting as a father to the whole Brotherhood. Let him have care of all things, and without the command of the Abbot do nothing. Let him take heed of all that is ordered, and not sadden his Brethren. But if any Brother shall perchance ask anything of him that is not reasonable, let him not, by contemptuously spurning, grieve him, but reasonable and with all humility refuse what he asks for amiss.

Let him have regard for his own soul, mindful of that rule of the Apostle: "They hat have ministered well, shall purchase for themselves a good degree." [173] Let him care diligently for the sick, the children, the guests, and the poor; knowing, without doubt, that for all these he shall give an account on the judgment day. Let him look upon all the vessels and goods of the Monastery as if they were the sacred vessels of the Altar. Let him neglect nothing; neither let him be covetous, nor prodigal, not wasteful of the goods of the Monastery, but do all things with moderation, and according to the command of his Abbot.

Above all things, let him have humility, and give at least a gentle answer unto him, on whom he hath nothing else to bestow; for it is written: "A good word is above the best gift." [174] Let him have under his care all that the Abbot shall appoint, and presume not to meddle with anything from which he shall forbid him. Let him give to the Brethren their appointed allowance of food, without arrogance or delay, that they be not scandalised; mindful of that divine word which tells what punishment he deserves "Who shall scandalise one of these little ones." [175] If the Community be large, let there be given to him helpers, by whose aid he may quietly perform the office committed to his charge. Let such things as are to be given or asked for, be given and asked for at suitable hours, that no one may be troubled or saddened in the House of God.

[173] I Tim. iii. 13..

[174] Eccli. xviii. 17.

[175] Matth. xviii. 6.

CHAPTER XXXII.

Of the iron tools, or goods of the monastery.

For keeping the iron tools, clothes, or other goods belonging to the Monastery, let the Abbot appoint Brethren, of whose life and conversation he may be sure, and to them let him allot all things to be kept, as he shall judge most expedient. Of these let the Abbot keep a list, that as the Brethren succeed each other in their various occupations, he may know what he gives and what he receives. If any one shall use the property of the Monastery in a slovenly or negligent manner, let him be rebuked. If he does not amend, let him be subjected to regular discipline.

CHAPTER XXXIII.

Whether monks ought to have anything of their own.

Especially let this vice be cut away from the Monastery by the very roots, that no one presume, without leave of the Abbot, to give, or receive, or hold as his own, anything whatsoever, either book, or tablets, or pen, or anything at all; because they are men whose very bodies and wills are not in their own power. But all that is necessary they may hope for from the Father of the Monastery; nor can they deep anything which the Abbot has not given or allowed. Let all things be common to all, as it is written: "Neither did any one say to think that aught was his own." [176] If any one shall be found given to this most wicked vice, let him be admonished once or twice, and if he do not amend, let him be subjected to correction.

[176] Acts. iv. 32.

CHAPTER XXXIV.

Whether all ought equally to receive what is needful.

As it is written: "Distribution was made to every one, according as he had need." [177] By this, we do not say that there should be accepting of persons, which God forbid, but that due consideration should be shown to each one's infirmities. Therefore, let him who needeth less, give God thanks, and be not grieved; and let him who needeth more, be humbled for his infirmity, and not lifted up for the mercy that is shown him; and thus all the members shall be in peace. Above all things, take heed there be no murmuring, by word or sign, upon any occasion whatsoever, If any one shall be found faulty in this respect, let him be subjected to most severe discipline.

[177] Acts. iv. 35.

CHAPTER XXXV.

Of the weekly servers in the kitchen.

The Brethren are so to serve each other, that no one be excused from the office of the kitchen, unless he be hindered by sickness or other business of more profit; because a greater reward is gotten thence. But let the weaker Brethren have help, that they may do their work without sadness; and let all generally have help according as the number of the Community, and the situation of the place, shall require. If the Community be great, let the Cellarer be excused from the kitchen, and as we have said before, such as are employed in matters of greater profit. Let the rest serve each other in charity. On Saturday, let him who endeth his week in the kitchen make all things clean. Let him wash the towels wherewith the Brethren wipe their hands and feet, and let both him who goeth out and him who cometh in, wash the feet of all. He shall hand over to the Cellarer, clean and whole, all the vessels of his office, and the Cellarer shall deliver them to him who entereth upon his office, that he may know what he giveth and what he receiveth.

Let these weekly Officers, one hour before refection, take each a draught of drink and a piece of bread over and above the appointed allowance, that at the hour of refection they may serve their Brethren without murmuring or great labour. Nevertheless, on solemn days let all forbear till after Mass. On Sunday, immediately after Lauds both the out-going and the in-coming officers for the week, shall cast themselves upon their knees before all, and ask to be prayed for. Let him that hath ended his office say the verse: "Blessed art Thou, O Lord God, Who didst help me, and console me," [178] which being thrice repeated, he shall receive the blessing. Let him who entereth upon his office follow immediately after and say: "O God incline unto mine aid, O Lord make haste to help me." [179] Let this likewise be thrice repeated by all, and having received the blessing, let him enter upon his office.

[178] Ps. lxxxv. 17.

[179] Ps. lxix. 2.

CHAPTER XXXVI.

Of the sick Brethren.

Before all things, and above all things, special care must be taken of the sick, so that they may be served in very deed, as Christ Himself, for He saith: "I was sick, and ye visited Me." [180] And "What ye did to one of these My least Brethren, ye did to Me." [181] But let the sick themselves bear in mind that they are served for the honour of God, and must not grieve the Brethren who serve them by their extravagant demands. Nevertheless, they must patiently be borne with, because there is gotten from such a more abundant reward. Therefore let the Abbot take special care they be not neglected.

Let a separate cell be set apart for their sue, and an attendant that is God-fearing, diligent and careful. As often as it shall be expedient, let the use of baths be allowed the sick; but to such as are in health, and especially to the young, let it be seldom granted. Moreover the sick and weakly may be allowed the use of flesh meat for their recovery. As soon, however, as they get better, they must all, after the accustomed manner, abstain from meat. Let the Abbot take special care that the Cellarer or attendants neglect not the sick, because whatever is done amiss by his disciples, is imputed to himself.

[180] Matth. xxv. 26.

[181] Ibid. 40.

CHAPTER XXXVII.

Of old men and children.

Although man's nature is of itself drawn to feel pity for these two ages, that is, for the old and for children, yet it is fitting that the authority of the Rule should provide for them. Let their weakness therefore be always taken into account, and the rigour of the Rule with regard to food, be by no means kept with them. Let a kind consideration be had for them, and let leave be granted them, to eat before the regular hours.

CHAPTER XXXVIII.

Of the weekly reader.

Reading ought not to cease while the Brethren eat at table. Neither ought anyone presume to read, who shall take up the book at haphazard; but let him who is appointed to read for the whole week, enter upon his office on Sunday. After Mass and communion, let him ask all to pray for him, that God may keep from him the spirit of pride. And let this verse be thrice repeated in the Oratory by all, the Reader first beginning it: "O Lord Thou wilt open my lips, and my mouth shall declare Thy praise;" [182] and thus having received a blessing, let him enter upon his duty. The greatest silence shall be kept, so that no muttering, or voice, shall be heard, except the voice of the Reader.

Such things as are necessary for meat and drink, let the Brethren so minister to each other, that no one need ask for anything. Yet should anything be wanted, let it be asked for rather by a sign than by a word. Nor let anyone presume to ask questions, about what is being read, or about anything else, lest occasion be given to the evil one. Should the Prior, however, think fir, he may make some brief exhortation for the edification of the Brethren. And let the Brother who is Reader for the week take a little pottage before he begin to read, on account of Holy communion, and lest perchance it be grievous for him to fast so long. Afterwards let him eat with the weekly Officers and servers of the kitchen. The Brethren must not read or sing in turns, but such only as my edify the hearers.

[182] Ps. l. 17.

CHAPTER XXIX

Of the measure or quantity of meat.

We think it sufficient for daily refection, both at the sixth and ninth hour, that there be at all seasons two dishes, because of the infirmities of different people; so that he who cannot eat of one, may make his meal of the other. Let therefore two dishes of hot food suffice for the Brethren, and if there by any apples or young vegetables, let them be added as a third dish. Let one pound weight of bread suffice for the day, whether there be one refection, or both dinner and supper. If they are to sup, let a third part of that pound be reserved by the Cellarer, to be put before them at supper.

If their labour be great, it shall be in the power of the Abbot to add what he shall think fitting to their ordinary allowance; taking care always to avoid surfeiting, that the Monks be not overtaken with indigestion, because there is not sin more contrary to a Christian than gluttony, as our Lord saith: "Take heed to yourselves lest perhaps your hearts be overcharged with surfeiting and drunkenness." [183] But to children to tender age, let not the same quantity be given, but less than to the older, in all things preserving frugality. Let all, except the very weak and the sick, abstain from eating the flesh of four-footed beasts.

[183] Luc. xxxi. 34..

CHAPTER XL.

Of the measure of drink.

Every one hath his proper gift from God, one thus, another thus." [184] Therefore it is not without some misgiving, that we appoint the measure of other men's victuals. Yet considering the condition of those in weak health, we think that one pint of wine will be sufficient for each one every day. But let those upon whom God bestows the gift of abstinence know, that they shall receive the proper reward. It, however, the situation of the place, labour, or the heat of summer, require more, let the Prior do what he thinketh good; ever having a care that fullness, or gluttony creep not in. And although we read [185] :that wine is not at all the drink of Monks," yet, because in these our times, they will not be so persuaded, let us at least agree to this, not to drink to satiety, but sparingly, "Because wine maketh even the wise to fall away." [186] Where, however, the poverty of the place will not allow the appointed measure, but much less, or perhaps none at all, let those who live there praise God and murmur not. This we admonish above all things, that there never be any murmuring.

[184] I Cor. vii. 7.

[185] In Vitis Patrum. Verba Senior: v. 4. 31.

[186] Eccli. xix. 2.

CHAPTER XLI.

At what hours the Brethren are to take their Refections.

From the holy Feast of Easter until Whitsuntide, let the Brethren take their refection at the sixth hour, and their supper at night. But from Whitsuntide, throughout the whole summer, let them fast on Wednesdays and Fridays till the ninth hour, unless they have to labour in the fields, or the extremity of the heat oppress them; but on other days let them dine at the sixth hour. This hour for dinner shall be continued at the discretion of the Abbot, if they have work in the fields, or the heat of summer be great. Let him so moderate and dispose all things that souls may be saved, and that what the Brethren do, may be done without just complaint. But from the thirteenth of September till the beginning of Lent, let the Brethren always take their meal at the ninth hour.

From the beginning of Lent till Easter, they shall take their meal in the evening; yet, let things be so ordered, that there be no need of lamps during the refection, but that all be done by daylight. At all times let the hour for supper and for dinner be so arranged that all things be done by daylight.

CHAPTER XLII.

That no one may speak after Complin.

Monks ought to keep silence at all times, but especially during the hours of the night; and therefore on all days, whether of fast or not, let them all come together, presently after supper if it be not a fasting-day, and let one read the "Collations," or Lives of the Fathers, or something else which will edify the hearers; nor, however, the Hepta-teuch, or Book of Kings, for it will not be profitable for weak under-standings to hear this part of Scripture at that hour; yet at other times it may be read. But if it be a fasting-day, let them, as we have said come to the reading of the Collations shortly after Even-song. Then let them read four or five pages, or as many as the time will allow, in order that during reading, all, even such as have had some work enjoined them, may have assembled together. All being gathered together, let them say Complin, after which no one shall be permitted to speak. If anyone shall be found to break this rule of silence, let him be liable to the most severe punishment; except there be some necessary cause, such as the arrival of guests, or the command of the Abbot. Yet, even in that case, let it be done with the greatest gravity and moderation.

CHAPTER XLIII.

Of those who come late to the work of God or to table.

As soon as the signal for Divine Office shall be heard, each one, laying aside whatever occupation he may happen to be engaged in, shall hasten with all speed, and yet with gravity, lest an occasion be given for light behaviour. Let nothing, therefore, be preferred to the Work of God. If any one shall come to Matins after the "Gloria" of the ninety-fourth Psalm, which we would have said slowly and leisurely for this very purpose, let him not stand in his order in the choir, but last of all, or in a place which the Abbot shall have set apart for such negligent people; that he may be seen by him and by all the rest, till the Work of God be ended, thus and do penance and make public satisfaction.

We have judged it fitting they should stand in the last place, or apart, for this reason; that being seen by all, they may for very shame's sake amend. For it they remain outside the Oratory, some one will perchance either return to his cell and sleep, or at least sit without, and, abandoning himself to idle talk, give an occasion to the evil one. Let him therefore enter in, that he may not lose all, and may be amended for the time to come. In the day Hours, let him that shall come to the Work of God, after the verse "Deus in adjutorium," and "Gloria" of the first Psalm, stand last, as directed above, and not presume to join himself to the choir of singers until he has made satisfaction, unless the Abbot shall, by his permission, give him leave; on condition, however, that he afterwards make amends for his fault.

He that cometh not to table before the verse, "Oculi omnium," or, "Edent pauperes," so that all may say the verse and pray, and all at once sit down to table together, shall be corrected once or twice, if this have happened through his own fault or negligence. And if he do not afterwards amend, let him not be admitted to a share of the common table, but being separated form the company of his Brethren, let him eat alone, and let his portion of wine be taken away from him, till be make satisfaction and amend his ways. He shall suffer the like penalty, who is not present at the verse "Confiteantur," or. "Memoriam," that is said after meat. And let not any one presume to take meat or drink before or after the appointed time. Moreover, if anything be offered to a Brother by the Prior and that Brother refuse it, but afterwards have a mind for it, he shall receive neither that, nor anything else, until he have made suitable atonement.

CHAPTER XLIV.

How those who are excommunicated, are to make satisfaction.

At the hour when the Work of God is being celebrated in the Oratory, let him, who for more grievous offences is excommunicated from the table or Oratory, lie prostrate before the doors thereof saying nothing; only with his head upon the ground, let him lie at the feet of all who go out of the Oratory. This he shall do until the Abbot think he hath given sufficient satisfaction. When ordered by the Abbot, he shall cast himself at the Abbot's feet, and then at the feet of all the Brethren that they may pray for him.

Then, if the Abbot shall order it, let him be received into the Choir, and stand in that rank which he shall appoint; yet so that he presume not to intone a psalm, or read a lesson in the Oratory, or do anything else unless the Abbot again order him. After each Hour, when the Work of God is finished, let him cast himself upon the earth in the place where he stands, and in this manner make satisfaction, until the Abbot commands him to cease therefrom. But let such as for slight faults are excommunicated only from the table, make satisfaction in the Oratory as long as the Abbot shall command, and let them continue their satisfaction until he bless them and say:--"It is enough."

CHAPTER XLV.

Of those who commit any fault in the Oratory.

If any one, while reciting a psalm, responsory, antiphon, or lesson, shall make any mistake and do not forthwith atone for it before all, let him be liable to greater punishment, as one who will not correct by humility, what he hath done amiss through negligence. But for such a fault, let children be beaten.

CHAPTER XLVI.

Of those who offend in lighter matters.

If any one, while engaged in labour, either in the kitchen or the cellar, or in the service of others, in the bakehouse, the garden, or in any other occupation, shall do anything amiss, or break or lose anything, or offend in any other say, and do not come presently before the Abbot or Community, and of his own accord confess and make satisfaction for his offence; when that is made known by another, he shall be more severely punished. But if the fault be a secret sin, let him manifest it to the Abbot only, or to his spiritual Seniors, who know how to heal their own wounds, and not to disclose or publish those of others.

CHAPTER XLVII.

Of making known the hour for the work of God.

Let the Abbot take care, both night and day, to signify the hour for the Work of God, either by announcing it himself, or by intrusting the duty of so doing to some watchful Brother, in order that all things may be done at their appointed times. But after the Abbot, let such as have been appointed, each in his own order, intone the psalms or antiphons. Let not any one presume to sing or read unless he have skill enough to do so, unto the edification of the hearers. Whomsoever the Abbot shall appoint to do this, let him do it with humility, gravity, and the fear of God,

CHAPTER XLVIII.

Of daily manual labour.

Idleness is an enemy of the soul. Therefore the Brethren ought to be employed at certain times in labouring with their hands, and at other fixed times in holy reading. Wherefore we think that both these occasions may be well ordered thus: From Easter till the first of October, let them, on going forth from Prime, labour at whatever they are required till about the fourth hour. From the fourth, till close upon the sixth hour, let them be employed in reading. On rising from table after the sixth hour, let them rest on their beds with all silence, or if perchance any one shall desire to read, let him read in such a way as not to disturb any one else.

Let None be said seasonable, at about the middle of the eighty hour, and after that let them work at what they have to do till the evening. If the situation of the place, or their poverty require them to labour in reaping their corn, let them not be saddened thereat, for then are they Monks in very deed, when they live by the labour of their hands, as our Fathers and the Apostles did before us. Yet let all things be done with moderation for the sake of the fainthearted.

From the first of October till the beginning of Lent, they shall be employed in reading till the second hour complete, when Tierce shall be celebrated, and from that till the ninth hour, let them labour at whatever work is enjoined them. At the first signal of the ninth hour, let them all leave off work, so as to be ready when the second signal is given. After their refection they shall be employed in reading spiritual books, or the psalms.

But in Lent they must read from morning till the third hour complete, then let them work till the end of the tenth hour, at what is enjoined them. In these days of Lent, let each one have a book from the Library, and read it all through in order. The books must be given at the beginning of Lent. Let one or two Seniors be specially appointed to go about the Monastery at the hours in which the Brethren are employed in reading, and see that no one be slothful or give himself up to idleness or foolish talk, and neglect his reading, being thus not only unprofitable to himself, but also a hindrance to others. If such an one be found (which God forbid!) let him be reprehended once or twice, and if he do not amend, let him be so severely corrected, that others may take warning by it. Neither let one Brother associate himself with another at unseasonable times.

On Sunday all shall devote themselves to reading, except such as are deputed for the various offices. But if any one shall be so negligent and slothful as to be either unwilling or unable to meditate or read, let him have some work imposed upon him which he can do, and thus not be idle. To the Brethren who are of weak constitution or in delicate health, such work or art shall be given as shall keep them from idleness, and yet not oppress them with so much labour as to drive them away. Their weakness must be taken into consideration by the Abbot.

CHAPTER XLIX.

Of the observance of Lent.

Although a Monk's life ought at all times to resemble a continual Lent, yet because few have such virtue, we exhort all in these days of Lent to live in all purity, and during this holy season to wash away all the negligences of other times. This we shall worthily accomplish if we refrain from all defects, and apply ourselves to tearful prayer, to reading, to compunction of heart, and abstinence. In these days, therefore, let us add something over and above to our wonted task, such as private prayers, and abstinence from meat and drink; let every one offer to God, of his own free will, with joy of the Holy Ghost, something above the measure appointed him; that is to say, let him withold from his body something in the way of food, drink, sleep, talk, laughter, and with spiritual joy and desire, await the holy feast of Easter. Nevertheless, let each one acquaint the Abbot with what he offers, and do it at his desire and with his consent; because whatever is done without the permission of the spiritual Father, shall be imputed to presumption and vain glory, and merit no reward. All things, therefore, must be done with the approbation of the Abbot.

CHAPTER L.

Of the Brethren who work at a great distance from the Oratory, or are on a journey.

The Brethren who work at a great distance; and, in the Abbot's judgment, are unable to come to the Oratory in due time, shall fall upon their knees in the place where they are labouring, and there perform the Work of God with divine fear. Also, those who are sent on a journey shall not allow the appointed hours to pass by, but perform them on the way as they are best able, and omit not to accomplish their task of Divine Service.

CHAPTER LI.

Of the Brethren who do not go far off.

Let not the Brother who goes forth upon any errand, and intends to return that same day to the Monastery. Presume to eat while abroad, even though invited to do so, unless perchance he has the Abbot's orders. If he do otherwise, let him be excommunicated.

CHAPTER LII.

Of the Oratory of the Monastery.

Let the Oratory be what its name signifieth, and let nothing else be done or treated of there. When the Work of God is ended, let all go forth with exceeding great silence, and let respect be paid to the presence of God, in order that the Brother who wishes to pray privately, may not be hindered from so doing by the misconduct of another. If any other Brother should also wish to pray secretly, let him enter without ostentation and pray, not with a loud voice, but with tears and earnestness of heart. Therefore, let not any one remain in the Oratory after the Work of God is ended, except for the purpose of prayer. Lest he be a hindrance to others.

CHAPTER LIII.

Of the manner of entertaining guests.

Let all guests who come to the Monastery be entertained like Christ Himself, because He will say: "I was a stranger and ye took Me in." [187] Let due honour be paid to all, especially to those who are of the household of the Faith, and to travellers. As soon, therefore, as a guest is announced, let the Prior or the Brethren go to meet him with all show of charity. First let them pray together, and so be associated to each other in peace. The kiss of peace shall not be offered till after prayer, because of the illusions of the devil. And in the salutation itself let all humility be shewn. By bowing the head or prostrating on the ground before all the guests who come or go, let Christ Who is received in their persons be also adored in them.

When the guests have been received, let them be brought to prayer, and after that, the Prior, or any one whom he shall order, shall sit with them. Let the Divine Law be read before the guest, that he may be edified, and afterwards let all courtesy be shown hem. For his sake, the Prior shall break the fast ordained by the Rule, unless perchance it be one of those special days, on which it cannot be broken. The Brethren, however, shall keep their accustomed fast. Let the Abbot pour water on the hands of the guests, and let both him and the whole Community wash the feet of the same, after which they shall say this verse: "We have received Thy mercy, O God, in the midst of Thy temple." [188] But let the poor, and strangers especially, be diligently entertained with all care, because in them Christ is more truly received. For the simple fear of the rich doth beget them honour.

Let the kitchen for the Abbot and the guests stand apart, in order that the latter, who are never wanting in a monastery, may not disquiet the Brethren by their untimely arrivals. Into this kitchen let two Brothers, who can perform its duties well, enter for a year. They shall have assistance when they need it, in order that they may serve without murmuring. When they have less labour, let them go forth to work where they shall be appointed. And not only in these, but in all other offices of the Monastery, let consideration be shown them, so that when they need help, it be given, and when they are without work, they obey and do what is commanded them.

Let the care of the guest-room be entrusted to a Brother, whose soul the fear of God possesseth. Let there be a sufficient number of beds there, and let the House of God be by wise men wisely governed. By no means let any one, unless appointed thereunto, either mix with, or speak to the guests; but if he shall meet or see them, after humbly saluting and asking their blessing, he shall pass on, saying that it is not lawful for him to talk with a guest.

[187] Matth. xxv. 35.

[188] Ps. xlviii. 10.

CHAPTER LIV.

Whether it be lawful for a Monk to receive letters or presents.

By no means let any Monk, without the Abbot's permission, receive from his parents or from anyone else, or give to another, letters, tokens, or any gifts whatsoever. And if anything be sent to him, even from his parents, let him not presume to receive it, unless it be first told the Abbot. If he order it to be received, it shall be in his power to appoint the person to whom it shall be given; and let not the Brother, to whom perchance it was sent, be grieved, lest an occasion be given to the devil. Whosoever shall presume to do otherwise, shall be subjected to regular discipline.

CHAPTER LV.

Of the clothes and shoes of the Brethren.

Let clothing be given to the Brethren suitable to the place where they live, and to the temperature of the air; because in cold countries more is needed, and in warm, less. The arrangement of all this shall be left to the discretion of the Abbot. Nevertheless we believe that for temperate places, it will be sufficient for each Monk to have a cowl and tunic: the cowl in winter to be of thicker stuff, but in summer finer and worn thin; also a scapular for work, and shoes and stocking to cover their feet. Let not the Monks find fault with the colour or coarseness of things; they shall be such as can be procured in the country where they live, or bought at the cheapest rate.

Let the Abbot take care of their dimensions, that they be not too short, but of a size suitable to those who wear them. On receiving new clothes, let them always give up the old ones at once, to be laid by in the wardrobe for the poor. For it is sufficient for a Monk to have two tunics and two cowls, as well for change at nights, as for the convenience of washing. Anything beyond this is superfluous and must be cut off. Also, they shall give back their shoes, and whatever is worn out, when they receive anything new. When sent on a journey, they shall receive drawers from the wardrobe, and on their return shall restore them washed clean. Let their cowls and tunics on such occasions be somewhat better than those they ordinarily use. They shall receive them on setting out, and restore them to the wardrobe on their return.

Let a straw mattress, a blanket, coverlet and pillow, suffice for their bedding. This the Abbot shall frequently examine, to prevent the vice of proprietorship; and if any one be discovered to possess anything which he hath not received from the Abbot, let him be subjected to the severest correction. To root out this vice, let all things be given them by the Abbot which shall be necessary, that is, a cowl, a tunic, shoes, and stockings, a girdle, a knife, a pen, a needle, a handkerchief, and tablets, that all pretence of necessity may be taken away. However let the Abbot always bear in mind that sentence from the Acts of the Apostles: "And distribution was made to every one according as he had need." [189] Let him, therefore, consider the infirmities of such as are in need, and pay no regard to the ill-will of the envious.

In all his ordinances let him always think on the retribution of God.

[189] Acts. iv. 35.

CHAPTER LVI.

Of the Abbot's Table.

The Abbot shall always take his meals with the guests and strangers. But as often as there are few guests, it shall be in his power to invite any of the Brethren he may choose. Let him take care, however, that one or two Seniors be always left with the Brethren, for the sake of discipline.

CHAPTER LVII.

Of the artificers of the Monastery.

If there be Artificers in the Monastery, let them exercise their crafts with all humility, provided the Abbot shall have ordered them. But if any of them be proud of the skill he hath in his craft, because he thereby seemeth to gain something for the Monastery, let him be removed from it, and not exercise it again, unless, after humbling himself, the Abbot shall permit him.

But if any of their work is to be sold, let those who make the bargain take heed and presume not to defraud the Monastery in any way. Let them remember Ananias and Saphira, [190] lest they, or any who defraud the Monastery, should incur the death of their soul, and these did the death of their body. And in the prices themselves, let not the vice of avarice creep in, but let things always be sold somewhat cheaper than by Seculars, that in all things God may be glorified.

[190] Acts. v. 10.

CHAPTER LVIII.

Of the manner of receiving Brothers to Religion.

Let not an easy entrance be granted to one who cometh newly to Religious life, but, as the Apostle saith: "Try the Spirits if they be of God." [191] If, therefore, the newcomer persevere knocking, and continue for four or five days patiently to endure both the injuries offered to him and the difficulty made about his entrance, and persist in his petition; leave to enter shall be granted him, and he shall be in the guest Hall for a few days. Afterwards he shall be in the Novitiate, where he shall meditate, and eat, and sleep.

Let a Senior who has the address of winning souls, be appointed to watch over him narrowly and carefully, to discover whether he truly seeks God, and is eager for the Work of God, for obedience and for humiliation. Let all the rigour and austerity by which we tend towards God be laid before him. And if he promise stability and perseverance, at the end of two months, let the whole Rule be read to him, with the addition of these words: "Behold the law under which thou desirest to fight; if thou canst observe it, enter in; if thou canst not, freely depart." If he shall still persevere, let him then be brought back to the aforesaid cell of the Novices, and be again tried in all patience. After the lapse of six months, let the Rule be read to him again, that he may know unto what he has come. If he still persevere, after four months, let the same Rule be read to him once more. If he shall then promise, after due deliberation, to observe all things and to do everything commanded him, let him be received into the Community, knowing that he is from that time forward under the law of the Rule, so that he can neither leave the Monastery nor shake off the yoke of the Rule, which, after so long a deliberation, he might have accepted or refused.

And when they admit him to profession, he shall, in the presence of all, make a promise before God and His saints, of stability, amendment of manners, and obedience, in order that if at any time he shall act contrariwise he may know that he shall be condemned by Him Whom he mocketh. He shall draw up the form of this promise in the name of the Saints whose relics are on the Altar, and of the Abbot there present. With his own hand shall he write it, or if he knoweth not how, another at his request shall write it for him, and the Novice shall put his mark to it, and lay it with his own hand upon the Altar.

After doing this, let him presently begin the verse: "Uphold me O lord according to Thy Word, and I shall live, and let me not be confounded in my expectation." [192] Let the whole Community repeat this three times, adding at the end, "Glory be to the Father." Then let the new Brother cast himself at the feet of all, that hey may pray for him, and from that hour he shall be counted as one of the Community. If he hath any property, he shall either first bestow it upon the poor, or by a formal gift, hand it over to the Monastery, without any reserve for himself; because for the future he must know that he hath not so much as power over his own body. Let him therefore presently, in the Oratory, be stripped of his own garments and be clothed in those of the Monastery. But the garments of which he is divested shall be kept in the wardrobe, that if (which God forbid) he should consent, by the persuasion of the devil, to leave the Monastery, he may be stripped of his habit and expelled. But he shall not have again the writing of his profession which the Abbot received from him at the Altar; that shall be kept in the Monastery.

[191] I John. iv. 1.

[192] Ps. cxviii. 116.

CHAPTER LIX.

Of the sons of nobles, or of the poor that are offered.

If any nobleman shall perchance offer his son to God in the Monastery, let the parents, if the child himself be under age, make the aforesaid promise for him, and together with the oblation [193] let them wrap that promise and the hand of the boy in the Altar Cloth, and thus dedicate him to God. But with regard to his property, they shall, in the said document, promise under oath, that they will never either give or furnish him with an occasion of having anything, either by themselves, or by any other person or means whatsoever. If they will not do this, but wish to offer something as an alms to the Monastery, by way of acknowledgment, let them make a donation of whatsoever they please, and reserve the income of it to themselves. Let matters be so managed that no expectation remain with the child, whereby being deceived he may perish (which God forbid). As we have learnt by experience in the case of others. Let those who are poorer act in the same way. But such as have nothing whatever, shall simply make the promise, and with the oblation give up their son, before witnesses.

[193] This was a host and a chalice in which there was some wine. The child held them in his hands during the ceremony of dedication. Constit: Lanfranci. Cap. xviii.

CHAPTER LX.

Of priests who desire to dwell in the Monastery.

If any one of the priestly order shall request to be received into the Monastery, let not permission be speedily granted even unto him. However, if he shall still persist in his request, let him know that he will have to keep all the discipline appointed by the Rule, and that no relaxation will be made in his favour, according to that which is written: "Friend, for what art thou come?" [194] Nevertheless he shall be allowed to stand next after the Abbot, to give the blessing, and to say Mass, provided the Abbot order him. Otherwise he shall presume to do nothing, knowing that he is subject to regular discipline, and particularly obliged to give unto all examples of humility. If his position in the Monastery shall have been given to him on account of his Order, or for any other reason whatsoever, let him remember that his true place is the one fixed by the time of his entrance, and not that which was yielded to him out of reverence for his Priesthood. But if any Cleric shall likewise desire to be admitted into the Monastery, let him be put in a middle rank, but only on condition that he promise observance of the Rule and stability in it.

[194] Matth. xxvi. 50..

CHAPTER LXI.

Of monks that are strangers, how they are to be received.

If any Monk who is a stranger shall come from distant places and desire to dwell in the Monastery as a guest, and being content with the customs he findeth there, doth not trouble the Monastery by his superfluous wants, but is satisfied with what he findeth, let him be entertained for as long a time as he desireth. And if he reasonable, and with loving humility, reprehend or point out any abuse, let the Abbot prudently take notice of what he saith; for the Lord hath perchance sent him for that very reason. But if, after a time, he should desire to take up his abode there, let him not be refused; especially since they had ample opportunities for discovering his manner of life, during the time he lived among them as a guest.

If, however, during that time he was found troublesome or faulty, not only shall he not be incorporated with the Community, but even be told with all civility to depart, lest others should be corrupted by his bad behaviour. But if he doth net deserve to be sent away, not only let him be received into the society of the community, when he makes the request, but let him even be persuaded to stay, that by his example others may be instructed; because in every place we serve one God, and fight under one King.

The Abbot may also put him in a somewhat higher rank, if he shall find him well deserving of it. And not only may the Abbot exalt a Monk to a higher place than is his due, but also any of the aforesaid Priests or Clerics, if their lives be such as to deserve it. Let the Abbot, however, beware never at anytime to receive a Monk into his Community from a known Monastery, without the consent of his Abbot, or letters of commendation from him, because it is written: "What thou wilt not have done to thyself, do not thou to another." [195]

[195] Matth. vii. 12.

CHAPTER LXII.

Of the priests of the Monastery.

If any Abbot desire to have a Priest or Deacon promoted to Holy Orders, let him choose from his Monks, one who is worthy to fill the office of Priesthood. But let him that is ordained beware of haughtiness and pride, and presume not to do anything except what is ordered by the Abbot; well aware, that he is now much more subject to the discipline of the Rule. Let him not, by reason of his priesthood, forget the obedience and discipline of the Rule, but rather strive to advance more and more in the service of God.

He shall, however, take his rank from the time he entered the Monastery, except in his office at the Altar, and also, in case the Community's choice and the Abbot's desire be to advance him higher for his holiness of life. He muse, nevertheless, observe the rules prescribed by the Deans or Provosts, and if he presume to act contrariwise, he shall be judged, not as a Priest, but as a rebel. If after frequent admonitions he do not amend, the Bishop shall be informed of his behaviour. If even after this he grow not better, and his faults become notorious, he shall be thrust out of the Monastery, provided his disobedience be such that he will not submit and obey the Rule.

broken. Let him bear in mind his own frailty, and remember that "the bruised reed must not be broken." [199]

By this, we do not mean that he should allow vices to grow up, but, as we have said before, with prudence and charity, seek to root them out in such a way as shall be expedient for each case; and let his aim be rather to excite love, than to inspire fear. He must not be truvulent and anxious; neither let him be over exacting, not headstrong, nor jealous, nor over suspicious, for then he will never be at rest. Even in what he orders, whether it pertain to God or to temporal matters, let him be prudent and considerate. Let him be discreet and moderate in the works which he enjoins, bearing in mind the discretion of holy Jacob who said; "If I shall cause my flocks to be overdriven, they will all die in one day." [200] Therefore adopting these and the like principles of discretion, which is the mother of all virtues, let him so temper all things that the strong may have somewhat to strive after, and the weak, nought from which they may flee away. Especially let him observe this present Rule in all things, that after having ministered well, he may hear from the Lord what the good servant heard, who gave corn to his fellow servants in due time; "Amen, I say unto you, over all his goods will he place him." [201]

[198] Matt. xiii. 52.

[199] Isai. xlii. 3..

[200] Genesis. xxxiii. 13.

[201] Matth. xxiv. 47.

CHAPTER LXV.

Of the Provost of the Monastery.

It often happens that by the appointment of a Provost [202] great scandals arise in Monasteries; because some, so appointed, being puffed up with the malignant spirit of pride, and esteeming themselves to be second Abbots, take upon themselves to tyrannise over others, to foster scandals, and to promote dissensions in the Community; and especially in those places where the Provost is instituted by the same Bishops of Abbots as the Abbot himself. How foolish this custom is, may easily be perceived; for a handle for pride is given to the Provost from the very beginning of his appointment, because his thoughts suggest to him that hie is now released from the power of his Abbot, since he is instituted by the very persons by whom the Abbot himself is instituted. Hence arise envy, quarrels, detractions, rivalries, dissensions, and disorders; and while the Abbot and Provost are at variance with each other, it must of necessity follow, that their souls are imperilled during this dissension; those also who are under their charge run to destruction by adhering, some to one side, and some to the other. The sin of this danger lieth principally upon those who were the authors of such an appointment.

Therefore, we foresee that it is expedient for the preservation of peace and charity, that the entire government of the Monastery depend upon the will of the Abbot. As we have before arranged, let all the business of the Monastery be transacted, if possible, by the Deans, according as the Abbot shall have determined, in order that, many being sharers in the same office, no one may become proud.

But if either the circumstances of the place require a Provost, or the Community with reason and humility ask for one, and the Abbot think it expedient, he shall with the advice of such of the Brethren as have the fear of God before them, nominate and appoint one himself. Let the Provost do with reverence what shall be enjoined him by the Abbot, in no way going against his will or ordinance; because the higher he is advanced above the rest, the more carefully ought he to observe all the precepts of the Rule. If the Provost be found viciously inclined, or deceived by the haughtiness of pride, or a contemner of the Holy Rule, let him be warned by word of mouth four times; if he do not amend, let the correction of regular discipline be applied to him. If with this he do not grow better, he shall be deposed from the dignity of the Provostship, and a worthier man put in his place. If after this he be not quiet and obedient in the Community, let him be expelled from the Monastery. The Abbot shall nevertheless bear in mind, that for all his judgments he shall have to give an account to God, lest perchance his soul burn with the flame of envy and jealousy.

[202] This corresponds to our Prior. St. Benedict uses Preaepositus and Prior synonymously..

CHAPTER LXVI.

Of the porter of the Monastery.

At the gate of the Monastery, let there be stationed a wise old man, who knows how to receive and to give an answer, and whose ripeness of age will not suffer him to wander from his post. He ought to have a cell near the gate, that such as come may always find him at hand, ready to give them an answer.

As soon as any one shall knock, or a poor man cry for aid, let him presently answer: "Thanks be to God," or invoke a blessing; and with all mildness of the fear of God, let him reply speedily in the fervour of charity. If he need help, he shall have a junior Brother with him. The Monastery ought, if possible, to be so constructed as to contain within itself all necessaries, that is, water, a mill, a garden, and a bakehouse; also that the various crafts be exercised within it, so that there be no occasion for Monks to go abroad, because it is in no wise expedient for their souls. We wish this rule to be frequently read in the Community, that no Brother may excuse himself on the score of ignorance.

CHAPTER LXVII.

Of brethren who are sent on a journey.

Let those who are to be sent on a journey commend themselves to the prayers of all the Brethren and of the Abbot, and always at the last prayer of the Work of God let a commemoration be made of all the absent. When they come back, they shall, on the very day of their return, lie prostrate on the ground of the Oratory during all the Canonical Hours, while the Work of God is being fulfilled, and beg the prayers of all, on account of the faults they may have committed on the way, by sight or hearing of evil things, or by idle discourse. Let no one presume to relate unto others what he has seen or heard outside the Monastery; because this is a fruitful source of evil. If any one shall presume to do so, let him be liable to the penalty prescribed by the Rule. In like manner shall he be punished who shall presume to break the enclosure of the Monastery, or go anywhere, or do anything, how trifling soever without leave of the Abbot.

CHAPTER LXVIII.

If a Brother be ordered to do impossibilities.

If any hard or impossible commands be enjoined a Brother, let him receive the injunctions of him who biddeth him with all mildness and obedience. But if he shall see that the burthen altogether exceedeth the measure of his strength, let him patiently and in due season state the cause of this inability unto his Superior, without manifesting any pride, resistance, or contradiction. If after his suggestion, the Prior shall still persist in his command, let the Brother know that it is for his good, and trusting in the assistance of God, let him obey through love for Him.

CHAPTER LXIX.

That no one presume to defend another in the Monastery.

Special care must be taken, that on no occasion one Monk presume to uphold or defend another in the Monastery, even though they be very near of kin. In no way whatsoever let any Monk presume to do this, because exceeding great occasion of scandal may arise from thence. If anyone shall transgress in this point, let him be severely punished.

CHAPTER LXX.

That no one presume to strike another.

Let every occasion of presumption be avoided in the Monastery. We ordain and decree, that no one, unless the Abbot hath given his authority, shall be allowed to excommunicate or to strike any of his Brethren. Such as trespass in this respect shall be reprehended in the presence of all, that the rest may be inspired with fear. But let all have strict discipline and care over children, until their fifteenth year; yet this also must be done with moderation and discretion. For he who shall, without the Abbot's leave, presume to chastise such as are above that age, or to be unduly severe even towards the children, shall be liable to regular discipline, because it is written: "What thou wouldst not have done to thyself, do not thou unto another." [203]

[203] Tob. iv. 16.

CHAPTER LXXI.

That the brethren be obedient to each other.

The service of obedience by all is not to be rendered to the Abbot only, but the Brethren shall also mutually obey each other, knowing that by this path of obedience they shall to unto God. Therefore, when the command of the Abbot, or of other Superiors constituted by him, have been first obeyed, (to which we suffer no private orders to be preferred), the Juniors shall obey their Seniors with all charity and diligence. If anyone be found contentious, let him be rebuked.

But if a Brother be rebuked for event he least thing by the Abbot, or by any of his Seniors; or if he shall perceive that the mind of his Senior is even slightly, be it never so little, moved against him, he shall, without delay, prostrate himself at his feet, and remain there till that commotion be appeased and he receive a blessing. If any one be too proud to do this, let him be liable either to corporal punishment, or if he prove contumacious, let him be expelled from the Monastery.

CHAPTER LXXII.

Of the good zeal which Monks ought to have.

As there is an evil zeal of bitterness which separateth from God, and leadeth to hell, so there is a good zeal, which separateth from vices and leadeth to God and life everlasting. Let Monks, therefore, exercise this zeal with most fervent love; that is to say, let them "in honour prevent one another." [204] Let them bear patiently with each other's infirmities, whether of body or of mind. Let them contend with one another in the virtue of obedience. Let no one follow what he thinketh profitable to himself, but rather that which is profitable to another; let them show unto each other all brotherly charity with a chaste love. Let them fear God, love their Abbot with sincere and humble affection, and prefer nothing whatever to Christ, and may He bring us to life everlasting. Amen.

[204] Rom. xii. 10.

CHAPTER LXXIII.

That the whole observance of perfection is not contained in this Rule.

We have written this Rule, that by its observance in Monasteries we may show that we possess, in some measure, uprightness of manners, or the beginning of a good Religious life. But for such as hasten forward to the perfection of holy living, there are the precepts of the holy Fathers, the observance whereof leadeth a man to the height of perfection. For what page, or what passage is there in the divinely inspired books of the Old and New Testament, that is not a most perfect rule of man's life? Or what book is there of the holy Catholic Fathers that doth not proclaim this; that we may by a direct course reach our Creator? Moreover, what else are the Collations of the Fathers, their Institutes, their Lives, also the Rule of our Holy Father Basil, but examples of the good living and obedience of Monks, and so many instruments of virtue? But to us who are slothful and lead bad and negligent lives, they are matter for shame and confusion.

Therefore whosoever thou art that dost hasten to the heavenly country, first accomplish, by the help of Christ, this little Rule written for beginners: and then at length thou shalt come, under the guidance of God, to those loftier heights of doctrine and of virtue, which we have mentioned above.

THE END.

Whosoever shall follow this Rule,

Peace on them.

Made in the USA
Las Vegas, NV
29 April 2023

71311786R10090